ROOTS
&
WINGS

Diego

ROOTS & WINGS

A Memoir of Hope and Transformation

Demetra Perros

Cover Art "Nike of Samothrace" by Rachel Brown Smith
Book and Cover Design by Rebecca A. Demarest
http://rebeccaademarest.com

This memoir presents research and ideas of its author. It is not intended to be a substitute for consultation with a health care professional. Most names and identifying details of people and places have been changed. The events portrayed herein have been relayed to the best of the author's knowledge.

The epigraphs from Euripides and Aristofanes have been translated by the author.

Performance photographs: © Meadowlark Images
Theatre photographs: © J. Nicholas Coffman

The fonts in this book include
CHARLEMANGE by Adobe
and **Athelas** by TypeTogether

Printed in the United States of America by createspace.com

*for Grace
and every artist
affected by trauma*

Roots & Wings mirrors the five act structure of dramas, reminiscent of Shakespearean plays and ancient Greek tragedies. This structure is based upon Aristotle's *Poetics*, as well as Northrop Frye's and Gustav Freytag's respective models.

PROLOGOS

They had to tether her to the ship's railing!

Everyone on deck wore chest harnesses. Sea legs usually took a week to acquire, but as the days passed, the swaying group thinned out, until I was the only one who gripped the railing. Hanging my head, I vomited over the side of the ship.

"You," a crewman barked. "You have to be strapped in." He looped the rope on my harness around the ship's railing and clicked the carabiner to the center of my chest. "You know how easy it is to fall into the water?"

The ship sliced through the waves.

If I fell overboard *here*, I'd be *that* far in just a few seconds. If I fell over *there*, I'd be even farther away. They wouldn't be able to turn the ship around. I'd be free. Enveloped in blue. Released from retching, from barking crewmen, from the reality of being stuck on this ship forever with no land in sight but the photos of Montana tacked to my bunk bed.

I leaned forward, craving the water.

Instead, my stomach constricted.

"You! Starboard!" another crewman yelled in a thick accent. He gestured to the other side of the deck. "There! Not here. You spill all over this ship."

"What?"

"The wind blow out that side. Go. Over there."

You care more about this ship than about the students, I wanted to yell back. But I had no fight in me. Feeling another upsurge of bile, I vomited over the railing.

Puke spilled onto the side of the ship.

I slumped over the bar. The harness tugged at my chest, binding me to the *SV Interlude* for an eternity.

ALPHA

Encroachment:
the overestimation of
ability and underestimation of risk

I

Now, be bold! Embroider your speech with gold.

~Aristofanes, *Wasps*

In ancient Greece, performers called upon the Muses, nine deities infused with inspiration. These nine sisters were borne of Mnemosyne, the goddess of memory. Mnemosyne helped performers preserve oral history by teaching them how to memorize. Through repetition, performers remembered thousands of lines of poetry that, when ready, they sang to audiences around the ancient world.

My own story ends and begins with nine. Nine days. Merged into a revolving mass of details and debris, these nine days have played through my mind for a decade now, singed into memory by repetition, by reliving an event that manipulated my past and inspires my present. Finally, after ten years of silently remembering, I am ready. Ready to share. But first, I need a little help:

Sing, O Muses, the passion of Demetra,
daughter of performance,
which brought shining triumphs
and haunting torments upon her journey.

Many a land did passion prompt her to traverse,
and many a stage did it entreat her to explore.
So now, O Muses, tell us her tale,
beginning where you deem most fitting.

And so, I begin.

My natural element was the stage. I began taking acting classes at the age of nine. I learned to speak clearly, to hold still, to always bring a pencil to class, and if you aren't ten minutes early, you're late. I grew up at Grandstreet Theatre in Helena, Montana. Grandstreet's darkened house felt like home. The smell of drying paint and sawdust was as familiar as the sweet scent of my mother's baklava. Ornate carvings decorated the ceiling, and velvet drapes hung from arched windows. A wooden proscenium framed the stage, in front of an auditorium that could seat up to 250 patrons. During rehearsals, the quiet atmosphere of the empty house exhilarated me. I liked seeing the chairs folded up, feeling that sense of possibility. What thrilled me most was a house full of people: expectant faces, murmuring voices, houselights dimming and stage lights rising. For ten years, I entertained the Helena community. For ten years, I was warmed by those lights.

At sixteen, I secured my first lead role: Abigail Williams in *The Crucible*. Fierce, pernicious, raging. The pinnacle scene was the opening of Act II, the woods, night. I entered onstage not in my drab gray dress, but clad in a mossy green shawl and white nightgown trimmed with just enough satin ribbon to be labeled indecent. Released from Puritan bonnet, my hair cascaded in dark curls, curls like tendrils that crept through the forest and circled around John Proctor's heart. I wailed. I told my John how Goody Johnson had pricked me in the back, how George Jacobs had wracked my arm, how I had pins and pricks all over my body. Reaching down, I slid the nightgown's hem up to my thigh. I tossed my hair back and laughed, knowing I had the full house and John Proctor in the palm of my hand.

Grandstreet Theatre produced several main stage shows each season. Kids, adults, and guest artists starred in the productions. Grandstreet also offered a summer camp and an after-school program, or theatre school, for third through twelfth graders. Every Christmas, the theatre school produced a play cast entirely with children. The Christmas show was directed each year by Charlotte Charles, the education director and theatre school mother of us all.

During my senior year of high school, I earned my first musical lead in a Christmas show. Charlotte cast me as Ida, the mother mallard in *Honk!* The musical retold the tale of the Ugly Duckling, complete with ponds, cattails, cat chases, and tap dancing frogs.

I enjoyed *Honk!* but felt spread thin because I was also juggling another play at my high school, maintaining a 4.0 GPA, serving as student body president, and preparing for a study abroad program second semester of my senior year: a tall ship, the ocean, and Southeast Asia as my classroom.

At theatre school one afternoon in December, Charlotte led announcements as usual. She reminded us about upcoming auditions and the annual Christmas dance. Before we separated into our respective acting classes, she invited me up to the stage.

"Jamie," she said, calling me by my American name, "tell us what you're doing after Christmas." I sat next to her on the edge of the stage, in front of third grade and high school theatre students.

"Well," I said to a row of children, "I'm going on an adventure, like Peter Pan in Never Neverland." Their faces rounded in glee. "My study abroad program is called Oceans Abroad. It's on a ship—not a cruise ship—but one with sails. Like Captain Hook's—*Arrr!*"

A little boy squirmed in his chair. "You gonna beat him?" he shouted.

"Captain Hook? You bet."

Gasps and *yeah!*'s broke out in the first few rows. Knowing smiles were exchanged between the high schoolers in the back and Charlotte and I in the front. "So how will you learn," she asked, "what with all that saving of Wendy to do?"

"I'll take classes on the ship," I said, "like English and history. I'll also have cultural projects at each port around Southeast Asia." I noticed the little ones' eyes start to glaze over. "I'll also learn how to climb the masts, so I can spot any mermaids with my telescope." I gazed up at the peaked ceiling. "I'm going to miss this place," I said, more to myself than to the theatre school. Grandstreet had transported me to other settings, other time periods, other realms. Theatre had shown me the world, but not the real world. Oceans Abroad would be my new portal. The wet deck my new stage. Not curtains, but canvas sails. Not backstage, but below deck.

Before wrapping up the theatre school announcements, Charlotte asked me one more question: "How'd you hear about this program?"

I looked into the audience and grinned. "From Emily's cousin."

Emily had grown up at Grandstreet too. She had a sharp ballerina profile and a voice that could trump any Disney princess's. We sang in the same choir at high school and performed in musicals together at Grandstreet. The summer before my sophomore year of high school, when we were in *Once on This Island*, she told me about a cousin who'd recently returned from a study abroad program on a sailing ship.

"I have to meet him."

Emily invited me to her house while her relatives were visiting. Her cousin, Gabe, had completed the program just over a year ago but still had that glint of adventure in his eyes. "It'll change your life," he told me over a bowl of yogurt and granola. We sat in the study, where he showed me the program's website. A 200-foot ship spanned the webpage, accented with quotes from students who'd sailed over the years. Oceans Abroad had been operating for nearly thirty years, accepting teenage students from around the world. The *SV Interlude* could hold up to seventy passengers: about fifty students, the rest crew and teaching staff. The ship had three masts, the tallest of which was thirteen stories high.

"If you pass the pull-up test," Gabe said, "you get to climb the masts."

"Pull-up test?" I asked.

"Five in a row."

I couldn't even do pull-ups in elementary school.

"You should really try to pass the test," Gabe said. "Most of my friends never did. I think they missed out. Being up there...it's like sitting on top of the world."

The more I listened to Gabe—the more I saw his cheeks glow and eyes shine—the more I wanted this maritime dream. I stared at the computer screen, longing for the salty wind and turquoise water. Sailing was in my blood, coursing from generations of seafarers.

My papou traveled the globe. During World War II, when the Nazis were occupying his quiet Greek village of Karystos, my grandfather escaped in the night on a small boat bound for Egypt. He earned his keep by working in the boiler rooms of ships. Eventually, he joined Greece's merchant marine service. An unconventional immigrant, he jumped ship and swam to America's shores. It wasn't until I was older—twenty-six, to be honest—that I learned the phrase is in fact an idiom. I thought he literally jumped off a ship and swam to New York, evading the Ellis Island officials notoriously known in my family for changing everybody's names.

The real story, as told by my Auntie Georgia, is that Papou was at port in Virginia in 1948. He left his station to visit his sister Sofia, who had moved from Karystos to Chicago sometime after the war. Surrounded by Greek culture and familiar looking faces in Chicago, Papou had an urge to anchor, to find a wife and marry. So my great-uncle Andy arranged a matchmaking event. Papou arrived at Sofia's house one afternoon to meet five women all lined up on a couch. He beheld Paraskevi and thought, *I hope this is the woman.*

That afternoon, as Paraskevi watched Constantino Perros play with his little nephew, she could "see in his eyes" that Papou was a good man. She would become my yiayia.

My grandparents settled in Chicago and soon had twins: my father and Auntie Georgia. Eventually, they moved to Duluth, Minnesota, to be closer to Yiayia's brothers. When my siblings and I were little, we used to sit on the shag carpet at our grandparents' house and listen to Papou's stories. In his thick Greek accent, he told us about haggling for fishing nets and holding his breath underwater while diving for sponges. Legs crossed, ponytail bouncing in delight, I knew that one day I would sail the world too.

Landlocked Montana offered vast skies and mountain ranges, but I always felt as though I didn't quite belong. I didn't know anyone else with dual names, I was darker and hairier than my friends, and I loathed winters—scraping ice off the car at six in the morning, applying layers of lotion onto chapped hands, having to wear snow boots underneath prom dresses in April. I couldn't wait to travel, go to college, go away. Grandstreet Theatre was the most diverse place in Helena, where I first heard American dialects and British accents. Books, too, transported me to different lands. I knew nothing about sailing, so I soaked up all the literature I could: *The Odyssey, The Iliad, Treasure Island, Moby-Dick.* "If I shall ever deserve any real repute," I memorized from Herman Melville's classic, "then here I prospectively ascribe all the honour and the glory to whaling; for a whale-ship was my Yale College and my Harvard."

When I met Emily's cousin, I knew I had found "my Harvard." Each year, Oceans Abroad announced a different itinerary, sometimes on the Mediterranean—which I was hoping for—other years around South America's Cape Horn, along northern Europe, or among the Polynesian Islands. When the program released its itinerary for spring 2004, I turned on the dial-up Internet at home and typed the website address.

Southeast Asia? I knew nothing about Malaysia or Brunei.

"Doesn't matter," Gabe told me over the phone. "Think of the range! You'll see third world countries, then powerhouses like Japan."

There was a lot to consider. The cost of the program seemed insurmountable. I didn't expect my parents to foot this—experiencing Oceans Abroad wasn't something I couldn't live without. It was a dream, something to believe in, regardless of whether it became reality or not. So I dreamed about the program for another year, all the while rereading *The Odyssey* and anticipating the release of Disney's *The Curse of the Black Pearl.*

The only way I could experience Oceans Abroad was through commitment and sheer effort. The program offered one full-ride scholarship—a single scholarship—that covered a semester's worth of tuition. My junior year of high school, while my friends were preparing college applications and theatre conservatory auditions, my eyes were on Oceans Abroad. I applied quietly, knowing I was competing internationally, against kids with stories a whole lot more exceptional than my own privileged American life. Gabe advised me to give it my all anyway. He said to find something I was passionate about and "showcase it" in my application. Well, that was simple: theatre, performing, acting and singing and dancing. I wrote my personal statement about the cultural diversity the world of theatre had exposed me to. My mother and I went to the print center downtown to make a colored booklet of photographs from the plays I'd been in over the years: *Anne of Green Gables, Big River, Godspell, A Christmas Carol, Once on This Island, West Side Story*, and a two-page spread of *The Crucible*. It was a beautiful book, my crown jewel of the performing arts.

Showcasing theatre in my Oceans Abroad application worked, enough to score an interview with Mr. Alfred, a man—*the* man—who handpicked students for the program. On an icy January morning in my junior year of high school, my mom drove me over a thousand miles to the interview.

I was escorted into an office. Mr. Alfred struck me as a serious man. He sat at his desk and beckoned me to sit down. "I know I look like an ogre," he said, chuckling. "But please, make yourself comfortable."

I stood in the doorway, hesitant to cross the threshold, feeling seventeen for the first time since believing in this dream. I knew nothing about boats and nothing about nautical navigation.

He wants to get to know you, Gabe's words floated through my head. I took a deep breath and walked into the interview the way I was trained to walk onstage: shoulders squared, chin lifted, and a confident expression on my face.

13

After covering the standard criteria—leadership roles, positive attributes, what can you offer the program—Mr. Alfred asked, "Where do you see yourself in ten years?"

"In ten years," I said, "I see myself living abroad. Greece, maybe... yes, Greece."

Mr. Alfred nodded for me to elaborate.

"I've graduated from college, and studied art history in grad school. I know the Greek language. I own an art gallery...in one of the island villages."

"And theatre?" he asked.

"Oh, I still return to Grandstreet every summer to teach at theatre camp."

As if smoking a mahogany pipe, Mr. Alfred took a long draw and studied the curious specimen before him. "You, Ms. Perros, are ambitious. I don't mean that in a negative way, but as a compliment of the highest kind."

I smiled, not entirely convinced it was.

Three days later, I was pulling into a parking spot at high school when my cell phone started ringing. It was my mom. Her voice sounded odd; either something bad had happened or something very out of the ordinary. "I just got a call from Oceans Abroad," she said. "You are the scholarship winner. You got the scholarship!"

"I did! I did?"

Mom explained that the program staff had tried to catch me before I left for school. "I know you'll just dance your way through today!"

Before stopping at my locker, I ran into my favorite teacher's room. "Mrs. Presley! They called!"

"Oh, my!" Mrs. Presley stood up from her cluttered desk to give me a hug.

I started crying.

"Oh, you! You're scared and excited."

"Yeah," I breathed. I couldn't quite comprehend the news.

"Here, do you have a tissue?" Mrs. Presley asked. "Take a handful for the road. Oh, I could tell when you walked into the room! We need to tie weights to your feet so you can stay on the ground with us."

During choir, Emily called out: "Everybody, Jamie has an announcement!" I told the fifteen girls I sang with every day. All fifteen of them ran down to the alto section to hug me.

A few days later, I parked my car in front of the state capitol building. It was my favorite spot in Helena, where I went at night after rehearsals to eat fries and chocolate milkshakes. I got out of my car and walked up the sloping lawn. The capitol was lit, fashioned with columns and a copper dome, a breathtaking monument to frontier history. Sitting on a bench, I stared into the night, finally understanding that I had received the scholarship. Excitement pricked the hair on my arms. I kissed my fingertips and released a blessing of thanks to the heavens. I, like my papou before me, would be sailing the wine-dark sea.

Seven months before starting Oceans Abroad, I visited Helena's county health department to find out what travel medicine I needed. Based on the tropical climates I'd be visiting, I was advised to get vaccines for yellow fever and typhoid fever, hepatitis A shots, and a TB skin test. The last form of prevention, an antimalarial, I wouldn't need until setting sail.

In January 2004, I visited Dr. Trent, my family's primary care physician. Over the years, Dr. Trent had charted my chicken pox, sore throats, and soccer bruises. He was retiring at the end of the month, but the receptionist squeezed me into his schedule. I showed Dr. Trent my itinerary, which included tropical regions infested with the deadly *P. falciparum* malaria strand. He consulted the Centers for Disease Control and Prevention, which recommended an antimalarial called mefloquine, a drug used to treat or prevent the infection of the *P. falciparum* mosquito parasite. Dr. Trent wrote me a prescription for Lariam, the brand name of mefloquine. Lariam was a pill taken orally on the same day each week. I was instructed to start the drug one to two weeks before setting sail, for the duration of my five-month trip, and four weeks upon returning to the United States.

On January 31, my family drove me to Helena's regional airport at 6:00 a.m. When we walked through the revolving doors, friends from high school and Grandstreet were already there to see me off. They clutched their coffees, tired but smiling. My older brother Nick and his girlfriend arrived in workout clothes. My little brother, Johnny, told me to take "a buttload of pictures." My sister Marika told me to check my enormous Oceans Abroad duffle bag when I landed for a "special gift" she and Mom had packed beneath my swimsuits. My dad handed me a red windproof pullover and told me to think of him when I wore it.

From Helena, I flew to Minneapolis, to Toronto, to London, to Kuala Lumpur, my last long layover before a few more legs to reach an outer island of the Philippines, where the *SV Interlude* was waiting to set sail.

Kuala Lumpur's airport reminded me of an intergalactic space station. The interior was white, the windows tinted black, and a tropical arboretum thrived in a central courtyard. I thought it a stark contrast: lush rainforest meets futuristic architecture. I couldn't tell whether the light in the arboretum was artificial or from the sun. I'd been traveling for over thirty hours and had no idea what the local time was. At one of the terminals, I met up with other Oceans Abroad students. They were disheveled, multi-accented, and weighed down with their own bulging duffle bags. Around twenty-five of us were fresh, new, second semester students. The other half had already attended fall semester on the ship and were returning to complete the rest of the school year. I clung to their stories as if they were reciting scripture. Finally, we boarded a small plane to the Philippines.

I have no recollection of inhaling the humid air for the first time, or of first beholding the ship docked in a harbor. The *Interlude* must've looked majestic, with its three masts shooting triumphantly into the sky. I imagine my heart beat in deep satisfaction. I like to think my mind has preserved this memory and that someday, I will be ready to relive that unbridled joy of oblivious youth.

I do remember that on the first evening, a group of us explored the island nightlife. We popped into a restaurant and were seated on an outdoor terrace. Vines wrapped around the railings and birds chattered on the rooftop. We ordered frothy drinks and entertained ourselves with existential discussion.

After we made our way back to the pier where the *Interlude* was docked, I found a quiet place on deck to take in the atmosphere. Leaning against the ship's railing, I peeked into the messroom. A few students were engaged in what looked like an intense poker game. Grinning, I looked down the length of the ship. The wheelhouse rose above the deck, and behind it, the classroom. I peered up at the masts. The canvas sails were tucked high up beneath the spars. I couldn't wait to see the sails full, billowing in the wind like the picture I'd seen on the website. My hair seemed to have doubled over the course of the muggy night, so I began gathering it into a bun.

"Hello," a hobbit-like voice said.

I looked up to see the bosun of the ship perched on a narrow set of stairs. He had round cheeks with brown stubble and an accent I couldn't quite place. We introduced ourselves. I gushed about how profound it was to gaze up at the masts.

His eyes twinkled. "A ship does make one philosophical," he mused. "It expands a mind." In his hand was a patch of leather with a needle plunged into it. The needle glinted in the lamplight. "Why, I've even taken up sewing."

"How crafty!"

"Not in the least." He chortled, shaking his head. We looked at what was supposed to resemble a pocket for his messenger bag. He explained how, once we were away from land, the stars would appear even brighter because we'd be completely free of light pollution. Gabe had said that too. *The stars,* he told me, *you'll see them for the first time out there.*

After the program's orientation in the Philippines, we set sail for Cambodia. The first port on our itinerary would take nine days to reach. That first evening at sea, the water was calm, the air warm. The ship's engine hummed quietly. I climbed a metal ladder to the roof of the classroom and watched the back of the ship create a wake in the foamy water. One of the teachers rested her elbows on the railing next to me. My skin itched, so I adjusted the collar of my green Oceans Abroad polo. "I'm starting to get these red bumps on my chest," I told her. She recommended I show them to the ship nurse.

The next afternoon, the staff held the long awaited pull-up test. After Gabe told me about it, I had started doing push-ups in my bedroom, and by this point, I had prepared for this test for over two years. My arms were strong, muscular, ready for the payoff. The new students gathered around a horizontal bar. One of the teachers explained how we had to grab the bar and complete five pull-ups in order to pass, just as Gabe had described. Most of the girls flat-out declined. When it was my turn, I stood directly below the bar, jumped to grab it, and pulled my body up—one, two, three, four, five times. My classmates cheered. Beaming, I dropped back to the deck.

The few of us who passed were taught how to harness ourselves into the system of ropes that extended up the masts. The staff told us we could go as high as we were comfortable. The ship was sailing smoothly on the water, so our climb would be stable. We cinched seat harnesses around our hips, tightened our chest harnesses, and secured ourselves into the rigging. I felt as though I was finally wearing the equipment of a real sailor.

At the foremast, I pulled myself up the rope ladder to the first set of sails. I continued up to the second set, where I paused to look down. My stomach tightened, but climbing into the sky outweighed any fear of heights. I crawled up to the third sail. Sitting back in my harness, I scanned the cobalt water. It stretched into the horizon and dissolved into a soft blue sky. Inhaling the salty air, my soul expanded to encompass the heavens and the sea. This was it—the pinnacle, to which all experience would be compared. Being suspended in air even trumped performing.

The fourth and fifth sets of sails towered above me. *I'll save those two for another day*, I thought to myself. Methodically, I inched my way down the mast. Lowering myself from the rope ladder, I descended into what would become my underworld.

Scene 1. Hives ravage my chest.

Scene 2. Ship nurse says, *Heat rash.*

Scene 3. Nausea.

Scene 4. Ship nurse says, *Seasickness. Just like everybody else.*

Scene 5. Vomit.

Scene 6. Vomit. Vomit. Vomit.

Scene 7. Enter dismantling of the mind.

Scene 8. Vomit.

Scene 9. Call parents from Cambodia. Say, *I'm coming home.*

II

You force me from this light. You make me bear such darkness.

~Euripides, *Ifigeneia in Aulis*

When my parents moved to Helena in the 1970s, their neighbors thought they were Colombian drug lords. My mom had teased hair. My dad had a thick mustache. Oh, and they were *dark*.

They met at a church social in Duluth, Minnesota. After my father graduated from pharmacy school, they left the Midwest to pursue job offers. It was late September when they visited Montana, an autumn with harvest moons, orange leaves, and warm nights. They fell in love with the rock-crowned mountains and historic homes. *What a perfect place to raise a family*, they agreed. A month later, they packed their car and drove a thousand miles west to Helena, where my father signed on with a local pharmacy. Eventually, he secured a government job at the VA hospital, where he worked the night shift.

Back then, Helena had a population of about 26,000 people. It was a town of prominent Irish Catholic families, perfect on the outside, yet each with a dresser drawer of flaws. Helena had no Greek Orthodox church, so my siblings and I grew up with tales of ancient Greek heroes instead of Bible parables. My parents tried to maintain as much of a connection to Greek customs as they could. They drove back to Duluth to baptize each of us in the church where they had met and married. In the Greek Orthodox tradition, my siblings and I were baptized with saints' names. I was named after Saint Demetrios. My older brother was named after Saint Nikolaos, my little brother after Saint Ioannis, and my older sister after the Virgin Mary, or Maria. In Greek, the diminutive form of Maria is Marika. In elementary school, classmates made fun of my sister's unusual name. "It's Ma-*ree*-ka," she corrected the kids with names like Kevin and Catherine and Paul. So my parents decided to call the rest of us by our American equivalents: Jamie, Nick, and John.

In the late '70s, my parents opened a restaurant downtown called Coney Island, where they sold hotdogs, gyros, and mini pizzas made on pita bread. The walls inside the restaurant looked bare, so my parents commissioned a local artist to paint murals of dancing hotdogs, clapping tomatoes, and a mandolin-playing gyro with my dad's black eyebrows and Greek nose. My childhood friends used to ask me which character I was on the walls. I could never decide between the hotdog girl with striped stockings or the grinning cucumber.

Coney was the only place in Helena where you could find lamb meat, Kalamata olives, and feta. The refined people of the capital refused to eat the lamb meat, so my parents reluctantly settled on a beef/pork blend. Now you pay, what, twenty dollars for a lamb burger? At Coney Island, state legislators, business owners, and Helena families lined the sidewalk for hotdogs and gyros. When I was little, I used to bus the booths. People left dimes and nickels—sometimes quarters even! The cooks started a tip cup for me behind the counter. After I cleared baskets and napkins, I proudly dropped my coins into the plastic cup.

My family never fit the typical Montana profile. While most mothers were lathering layers of SPF 50 onto their children's fair skin, my mom was tanning next to our plastic kiddie pool. My dad was the only one of my friends' fathers who wore shorts all year round. He also engaged in gastronomic business deals. He paid for my braces by bartering Greek-village-style: free gyros for life in exchange for his daughter's flawless smile. When he wasn't working at the pharmacy, Dad drove a golf cart converted into a mobile food stand. Sometimes he picked me up from elementary school in the hotdog cart. I never felt embarrassed because my dad was "*the hotdog guy!*"

My parents divorced when I was in second grade. What had once been a golden childhood of endless summers playing in the backyard soon became a hectic cycle of carting toys and clothes between two parents' houses. Helena, which had once been united in my eight-year-old mind, seemed divided. My parents had an ugly, public divorce. Suddenly, people were only friends with one parent and not the other. I didn't know how to talk about Mom without my dad getting mad. I didn't know how to talk about Dad without my mom getting mad. Ever the crowd pleaser, I didn't want to make either one upset, so I bottled my emotions and eventually released them through the characters I played onstage. Like Abigail Williams in *The Crucible*, because of my wild hair. Or a Shark in *West Side Story*, because of my tan skin.

Three years after the divorce, Dad sold Coney Island. "Because," he told me, "this place has too many memories." I was sitting on top of the chest freezer, by the pita breads we were prepping for the next day. Dad ladled homemade pizza sauce onto each pita. As I carefully arranged the pepperonis—five around the border and one in the center—I remember thinking about the memories I had of Coney. They were all happy ones. In time, I came to understand that happy memories are the ones that can make you the saddest.

Eventually, Dad moved to a house on a lake about twenty miles from Grandstreet Theatre. Mom moved to a house in the Elkhorn Mountains about twenty minutes from high school. My siblings and I rotated between the two homes, while trying to keep Helena as the hub. By my senior year of high school, my older siblings had dispersed. Nick lived in town, and Marika was splitting her time between America and Germany. When my own time came to leave, I was prepared, eager. But I hadn't planned on coming back so soon.

I returned from the ship on February 17, 2004, less than three weeks after embarking. It was February 17 for two days: once in Cambodia where I boarded the plane, and again when I crossed the international date line and flew into LAX. I remember very little about the flights from Asia to Helena. Just a few details that became significant over time.

At LAX, I bought a plain bagel and a drink. I remember being overwhelmed by the choices—pop, water, milk, tea, juice. The bottles lined the countertop. Lightheaded and weary, I was afraid I'd bump into one and send them all crashing to the floor. Stepping away from the counter, I pointed to a lemonade and said, "This."

It was the first time I had spoken since being escorted in Taiwan to a connecting flight. When I purchased my ticket, Oceans Abroad had to attest that I was able to travel. On February 15, the ship nurse and program director drove me to a travel agency in Cambodia. The travel agency was located in a mall, near a food court. I remember smelling the fried noodles and feeling ravenous. The program director talked to a woman. I sat hunched over on a chair while they discussed my flights. A glossy map of the world spanned the wall. I traced the remaining course of the *Interlude*. I stared at each country, wondering what I'd be missing.

"Is she fit to travel?" The curt voice of the agent interrupted my thoughts. She took in my matted hair and the stains on my unzipped pullover. Her eyes lingered on my chest, which was covered in red blisters. It seemed as though a visual test was being conducted, and the only way I could go home was if I passed. I smoothed my hair and rolled my shoulders back, trying to sit with good posture. I zipped up my red pullover and attempted to smile, but my lips stretched tightly over my teeth. An image of a grinning skeleton flashed in my mind.

The program director told her I had been seasick for nine days. The ship nurse confirmed I would be able to fly home. The travel agent explained that someone would escort me to the gates at the airports in Cambodia and Kuala Lumpur. "For your weakness," she said. I dropped my shoulders, relieved I had passed the test. I didn't know it then, but that word, *weakness*, would follow me back to the States.

I remember eating my snack somewhere in LAX. The bagel was soft, the lemonade tart. I stopped drinking it because my mouth began to sting. My gums felt hot on my tongue. I cleaned the lenses of my bent eyeglasses and read the entire label on the lemonade bottle. I read it to block out images I had of vomiting on the floor in my bunk room. The lemonade company was started by a couple of guys— brothers?—somewhere on the East Coast. I kept rereading the label, thinking I could distract my mind.

The next thing I knew, I was walking on the tarmac of Helena's small airport. The hem of my pants kept catching under my shoes, so I lifted my jeans by the belt loops. I wore a brown scoop neck blouse. It was winter, but the cold air on my arms felt good. My black Mary Janes crunched on the snowy concrete. The shoes were supposed to be worn with my Oceans Abroad uniform as we greeted consular staffs in tropical harbors, not as I walked in icy weather back through the same doors I had passed less than three weeks ago.

"There she is," I heard Nick say.

My mother held my shoulders. "I didn't recognize you," she said, more to herself than to me. Her hands wrapped the circumference of my upper arms, arms that not a month ago had passed the pull-up test. "You're so tiny. *My Jamie Baby.*"

I should have cried then, in the embrace of my mother. Or after my father ruffled my hair as he always did, or when Nick engulfed me in a muscular hug. But I didn't feel anything, just my shirt as my dad examined the rash on my chest, just my jeans as my mom tugged on them and remarked how thin I was, just the sores in my mouth that were getting hotter.

I knew I had been somewhere far away, but now I was back in my room, lost in the ivy pattern of my bedspread with my teddy bear, Kirby. Huge blankets covered my mind, obscuring my ability to remember. It all seemed surreal, like it had never happened. But every time I tried to sleep, I was reminded that it had. When I closed my eyes, my head spun and my stomach plunged up and down as it had below deck. So I kept them open. I traced the vines across the bedspread. I pulled the drapes open late in the night. Moonlight shone over the peaks of the Elkhorns. I couldn't understand why I didn't see water reflecting the moon or sailboats docked under lamplight. I tried to make sense of where I was until I noticed a sports drink next to me. There weren't any sports drinks on the ship, so I knew I must be home.

There wasn't anything on the ship to curb dehydration, no motherly remedies of chicken broth, no electrolyte-replenishing drinks or popsicles. "Then how are we supposed to get better?" I yelled at the ship nurse one day. She sent me up to the messroom with the other students who had overcome their own seasickness, who were chatting and joking and sipping their minestrone soup. I took a seat on the bench and tried holding my spoon steady, hoping not to spill on my lavender tank top. It was the tank top I'd worn the day I passed the pull-up test. I had not taken it off since.

I felt the stares, saw them. I heard the whispers, believed them. A boy smiled sympathetically at me from across the table. Some girls eyed my unchanged clothes and clumped hair. But I couldn't be bothered by my appearance. I had more pressing issues to overcome, like how to navigate between the packed benches and through the narrow doorway that opened to the deck so I could expel the acidic sludge creeping up my throat. I reached the railing just in time. Gripping it, my knees buckled, and I vomited over the side of the ship. Wiping my mouth with the back of my hand, I turned to look through the doorway at my healthy peers.

When I returned, my father set up a series of doctor appointments. First, my parents took me to a dentist, who examined the sores in my mouth. "Your gums have pulled away from your teeth," the dentist said. The constant vomiting had kicked up too much stomach acid, which was eating away at the soft tissue in my mouth. He filled my gumline with a brown glaze. Then he gave me a soft-bristled toothbrush, toothpaste for sensitive teeth, and my pick in the treats drawer. I chose a plastic parachute man and a sticker that read *Super!*

Next, my parents took me to a dermatologist. "This rash is an adverse drug reaction to Lariam," the dermatologist said.

"My antimalarial?"

The dermatologist's diagnosis was confirmed by a primary care physician. Since our long-standing family doctor had just retired, my dad arranged an appointment with a different provider, a woman named Judith Pitney. My parents accompanied me into an exam room.

I flopped onto the exam table. Dr. Pitney checked my mouth and torso. "When did you take your most recent dose of Lariam?" she asked.

"Today."

"*Today?*" she and my dad asked in unison.

My breaths quickened. "I'm supposed to take it four weeks upon returning to America." My head pounded. "Today is Wednesday. I take it every Wednesday."

Wednesday, January 21.

Wednesday, January 28.

Wednesday, February 4.

Wednesday, February 11.

Wednesday, February 18.

Five doses total.

"You took it on the ship?" my mom asked.

"Yes." I had felt proud of myself that despite being sick, I was still a responsible international traveler who took my pills. As prescribed.

"Stop taking it," Dr. Pitney said. She turned sharply to my parents. "Had she stayed on board, she could've died from dehydration."

The three of them discussed hospitalization and hooking me up to an IV.

I shook my head *no*.

"Fine," Dr. Pitney said. She instructed my mother to buy electrolyte drinks and give me as many liquids as possible. "Juice, water, popsicles—anything she can keep down."

My parents helped me down from the exam table. "I thought I had heat rash," I said to them, "and seasickness. That's what they told me on the ship."

I wanted details, answers, but Dr. Pitney hadn't spent any time on the effects of the antimalarial. She, like many health care professionals in 2004, was unfamiliar with the drug.

At the pharmacy where my father worked, he printed out pages and pages listing side effects of Lariam. He told me to circle any that I had been experiencing. In my bed, I went through the packet, highlighting nearly every line, finding words for what I had been told by the ship nurse was seasickness: fatigue, loss of balance, dizziness, nausea, vomiting. I also found words for side effects I hadn't told anyone I'd experienced on Lariam: anxiety, paranoia, and hallucinations.

In ancient Greek, the word for pharmaceutical drug is φάρμακον (pharmakon). It means a remedy and a curse.

Nearly a decade afterward, I asked my mother about my homecoming. This was the first time I gave anyone permission to talk about Oceans Abroad. We set up a phone date, she collected some notes over the week, and on a Thursday evening, I shut the door to my study.

"I got a call from you in Cambodia," my mother told me over the phone. "You said, 'Don't be afraid when you see me, because I look different.' I remember I cried then. I mean—what does that mean?"

She paused, and in those few seconds, I tried to fathom what it must've been like for a mother to get a call like that.

"You flew back on February 17," she continued. "At the airport, you were wearing jeans, a dark top, hair pulled up. You looked like you were eight years old. You were still Jamie, but your color was off. Jaundiced. And there were these blisters and sores on your chest. I think you were more concerned about how we felt, seeing you come off the plane in that condition."

Sometimes I wonder if my imagination has embellished my return, but no. We both remember what I was wearing. I really had lost that much weight. My rash really was that noticeable. Yet some details I don't remember. She said that when she brought me home, I went straight to bed. "You didn't want to take a shower. The water reminded you of the ship."

28

"I didn't shower? Really?" I pressed the phone to my ear, not wanting to miss a piece of the mosaic.

"You had vomit in your hair."

"I remember that."

"You were a matted mess. My drooling Jamie."

We laughed.

My habit of drooling was nothing new. When I was little, I used to crawl onto Dad's chest as he sat in the family room watching golf highlights. Within five minutes I'd be out, and within eight, he'd have a circle of drool soaking into his polo shirt.

"You wouldn't show me your clothes," Mom said. "Finally, you let me open that duffle bag. I took your laundry out in the sink one by one. Chunks. They were covered in chunks."

She shouldn't have had to touch that stuff. I should've left all of it there, especially that red pullover.

One night on the ship, I was on the list for night duty. I'd been below deck for what seemed like months, but I didn't protest. If the other students could perform night duty, so could I. My eyes were too dry for contacts, so I put on my glasses and grabbed the new red pullover Dad had given me. The tag described how it could slice through wind and rain.

On deck, the waves were mounting and spilling onto the ship. I was ordered to retrieve a pile of rope. I ran, trying not to slip on the wet deck. As I reached down, my glasses fell off. Fumbling in the sea spray and darkness, my hands searched.

"The rope! Come on!"

I was torn between recovering my sight and fulfilling a command I so desperately wanted to get right. As I stepped closer to the pile, my shoe skidded on something round. I bent down, trying to pick up both the soaked rope and my cracked glasses. By then, the crew and other students had rushed over to the pile, heaving the rope in a collective unit. As I watched them, puke spilled down my front. The red pullover clung to my shaking body, its fabric unable to protect me from humiliation.

Between the tears and the vomit, I contributed not even a hand.

"You couldn't look at your clothes." My mother's voice jolted me back to the present. "I brought them upstairs, all clean and folded. I was putting them away in your closet when you woke up. 'Get them out!' you yelled. They—they haunted you."

I had her throw them away: the raingear, the button-down uniform, that red pullover. They reminded me of everything I had failed to accomplish.

"You were so used to excelling, following through on everything you set out to do. This was the first time in your young life that you couldn't, from start to finish, complete something. In your mind, that was very hard to accept as okay."

A perfectionist, I've been called. An overachiever. Perfectionists may look like they have their priorities straight, but they don't. Perfectionists should actually be watched the closest because we are some of the harshest self-critics. Before the ship, my self-criticism had been fuel for improvement; it had motivated me to be better than myself. After the ship, self-criticism didn't raise me up. It beat me down.

I asked my mother about the weeks before I returned to high school. "You sweated a lot. Slept a lot. You were absolutely exhausted. Your body had to get rid of all those toxins before it could begin to heal. You'd sleep for hours, days. 'Jamie, you've got to get some electrolytes. A popsicle, anything.' You weren't eating that much to begin with, only small portions. But you couldn't keep food down. You'd wake up so hungry, but you couldn't keep up with your hunger."

She paused, and I tried to recall this period of time, but nothing, no memories emerged.

"You had that issue for a while. If it wasn't coming out one way, it was coming out the other. But mostly out of your bottom. Your diet had changed so drastically that I didn't know what to feed you."

I don't remember the hunger. I don't remember the sweats. I don't remember that I avoided showering and sleeping in the dark. Of all the details I don't remember, the one that makes me the saddest is about a pillowcase. It was lavender, and it had a twin. On the corner of each pillowcase, my mother had embroidered two hearts: one for me, and one for her. She used her pillowcase at home, and she told me that I took mine with me on the ship. They would be our way of staying close while I was at sea.

"What color were they?" I asked her on the phone.

"Lavender."

"And the sheets?"

"Lavender, too. We bought them together, remember?"

I racked my brain, probing for the fabric. I usually remembered colors, if nothing else. But I couldn't. I couldn't remember the pillowcases. "Where were the hearts? Were they cross-stitched? Are you sure?" The more she described the pillowcases, the emptier my brain became. Why, out of the handful of memories I do recall, couldn't one of them be about the love of my mother? Couldn't I have kept just this one?

After talking for over an hour, I grew weary. Mom seemed grateful to end the conversation too. It was exhausting, remembering and not remembering. That night I lay in bed, demanding my brain to extract the lavender pillowcase. It hasn't yet.

Shortly after I returned from the ship, my mother called my high school guidance counselor, Mrs. Lambert. She told my mother that I didn't need to rush back into school. She would "take care of it." From their phone conversation, I overheard that the administration had discussed whether or not I could even graduate because I had missed so many days of school. My situation was compared to a student dropping out of high school and then reenrolling. The argument had to do with numbers and federal funding.

From a community where I had excelled, I felt rejected.

When Mom got off the phone, I pretended as though I hadn't heard. "How'd it go?" I asked.

She smiled. "Mrs. Lambert is taking care of everything."

I smiled back, but felt no happiness.

About a month after returning from the ship, I drove myself to high school. I parked in the same lot where a year ago I had received the call about the Oceans Abroad scholarship. I walked through the doors to my locker, my ears keen on picking up any rumors about why I was back. I was still trying to make sense of it myself. *I got sick*, I practiced to myself. *I got really sick. I had a bad reaction to Lariam. Lariam is like a vaccine for malaria.* But they all sounded like excuses. I was back because I couldn't cut it. I had returned to my hometown a disappointment. I had failed to do what my ancestors had done for thousands of years before me and what each of my grandparents did to arrive in the new world: sail the wine-dark sea.

On that first day back at school, I was walking in the hallway when my locker neighbor slammed her locker shut. "*Gah!* I just told off some chick for talking smack about you. She said you got kicked off the ship, but I told her that you were really sick."

I turned the dial of my lock, one number at a time. "Thank you."

"Are you kidding? People are morons!" She yanked her locker open and threw her books onto the shelf. I filed a notebook into my own. I appreciated her fervor, but didn't have the energy to match it.

Still dehydrated, I toted around a one-quart water bottle. I used that water bottle as proof that I had indeed been sick. But my body showed as much without it. My midriff sunk inward, my arms were thin, my butt swallowed by jean pockets. I was no longer a curvy mermaid; I was a withered stem of kelp.

I also overheard I was anorexic.

At school, I used to chat with friends in the hallways and actively participate in classroom discussions. When I returned, I avoided social interactions. My friends asked me to join them for lunch. I always politely declined. Instead, I left school to work out at an athletic club nearby. When I got off the ship, I weighed just over 100 pounds. Looking thin made me feel weak, vulnerable. I needed to regain my muscle mass. I needed to rebuild an image of glory, to at least look invincible.

After my workouts, I'd drive back to school. I sat in my car and chewed the sandwich my mother packed me. I gazed at the cursive

Jamie on my lunch bag. I used to believe that handwriting belonged to the Tooth Fairy. By the end of March, paper bags carpeted the passenger seat floor, banana peels and empty baggies spilling out of them.

Nine years later, I called one of the few high school friends with whom I've remained in contact. Her name was Steph, and she had been the student council treasurer our senior year. We had spent many early mornings decorating the gym for homecomings and winter formals. As teenagers, we had both felt as though Montana couldn't quite contain us, couldn't quite house our dreams. "I was so jealous," Steph laughed on the phone. "Jamie's getting out. Honestly, that's all I wanted to do. Get out of Helena. I remember your program ran into summer, then you'd be off to college. You were getting this jumpstart on life after Montana."

Steph had been at the airport when I flew out. "You were ready," she recalled. "Smiling. Normal Jamie. Just so excited. You were going on your odyssey, your initiation into adulthood, so to speak."

When I returned abruptly to high school, Steph had approached me in the hallway and asked about a check the student council had given me as a going away present. I was taken aback. "I had to spend it on my plane ticket back to America," I told her. At the mall in Cambodia, I had to cash my traveler's checks so I could afford to fly home. I didn't know if Steph was expecting me to return the money or if the council was asking for it back. I felt ashamed. I felt kicked out of the club that I had belonged to for almost four years.

On the phone, I asked Steph if there was ever a discussion about me returning to student council. "I'm trying to remember if there was," she said. "Everyone knew, those first few weeks, that you were back but were sick at home. I don't remember. There probably wasn't. You made the choice to leave. We moved on. When you did come back to school, I know your vice president and I talked about it. Not much came of that discussion."

I asked Steph what she remembered about my return to high school. "You came back," she said, "but you didn't. It was as if you were still gone. Kind of like a ghost. You just had this sadness about you. That positive, happy Jamie wasn't there. When you were around, you were kind of limited. Emotionally, physically."

Steph and I had been in the same chemistry class first period during fall semester. When I returned, I couldn't catch up on almost two months' worth of chemistry equations, and I was having trouble waking up in the morning. I saw our chem teacher in the hall one day. "Hey," he barked. "Why aren't you back in class?" I mumbled a reply about needing to take it easy. My answer didn't seem to satisfy him, and a fresh wave of failure washed over me.

"I wanted to be there for you," Steph continued, "but I didn't know how. And you weren't there to be. You weren't in chem anymore, we weren't table buddies, I didn't see you at lunch. It just felt like you were gone, one hundred percent gone. I knew it was tough for you to come back, to have to look at people and think that you failed. You didn't. But you had this overwhelming feeling that you had. I remember being so sad about that. I didn't know what to do about it, how to talk about it, how to fix it. I remember thinking, *I'm concerned about Jamie, having these health issues, but I feel like I've lost a really good friend. I feel like she doesn't want to hang around me anymore.* We were typical teenagers," she said about herself and our friends. "We didn't want to make the situation worse for you. It's not that we weren't thinking of you or didn't want to reach out— it's that we didn't know how to have an emotional conversation." She paused. "It was just one big ball of suck."

I laughed. "Well said."

"I'm sorry if you ever felt abandoned by us," Steph told me on the phone.

I tried to find the right words. "I'm sorry—too. That you felt like I didn't want to be your friend." My words sounded juvenile, inarticulate, like an eighteen-year-old had spoken them.

III

Artemis demands my body.

~Euripides, *Ifigeneia in Aulis*

Every Friday in AP English, a student brought in music lyrics and led a close reading of the text. On my Friday, I printed off a song from the musical Chicago. "The song," I said above the whir of the projector, "isn't in the film version, but it plays during the closing credits. You have to wait for the words because the vamp is so long."

Last semester, I would've stood tall in front of the class, looking everyone in the eye. Now my eyes remained on the lyrics. The laminated sheet stuck to my fingertips. "I chose it because...it helps."

Expectant faces stared up at me: girls from choir, boys I'd grown up with at Grandstreet Theatre. I thought they were waiting for me to offer a sliver of what I'd been through on the ship. "I'll let the song speak for itself," was all I said.

The class waited through the minute-and-thirty-second vamp. It was important that they waited. That was part of the song's message.

At last, the first verse opened with Velma Kelly's deep, velvety voice. Then Roxie, in a raspy lilt, added her two cents.

At the front of the classroom, I kept my lips pressed, careful not to reveal a smile, a frown, any hint of emotion. But at lunchtime, in the privacy of my car, I whispered with Velma and Roxie the words to "I Move On."

It started in April. Grandstreet Theatre was planning its annual showcase for graduating seniors. Students were required to perform classical monologues. After school, I drove home before my mom and little brother returned. In the empty house, I positioned a dining room chair out to a pretend audience. My monologue was from the ancient tragedy *Ifigeneia in Aulis*, by Euripides. In the play, King Agamemnon's fleet can't set sail for Troy until he sacrifices his daughter, Ifigeneia, to the goddess Artemis. In the monologue, Ifigeneia tries to convince her mother that she doesn't mind being sacrificed to the sea so her father can launch his ships for Troy. "Nothing's new or changes," I rehearsed. *What does that mean?* I thought to myself. "Nothing's new or ch—"

Nothing changes.

I'd try to finish the monologue, but I always returned to that line until one day, it happened. It felt like my chest was cracking open, like a terracotta jar splitting into a thousand shards. My eyes filled with water and when I blinked, I was drowning in tears.

After that first afternoon, crying became easier. Every day after school, I rehearsed until Ifigeneia's grief merged with my own. Tears streaked our cheeks. I knew what she was crying over: her lost dreams of marriage, of motherhood, of living a full life. But I couldn't articulate what I was missing. I just cried.

After the showcase in May, I stopped rehearsing. So I stopped crying. I pieced my chest back together and fastened a shield over my heart.

When he was little, my brother Nick used to stack towers of blocks in the living room. Mom said that from the kitchen she'd hear: "Okay, Ma! Set 'er loose!" She'd place me in the middle of

Nick's miniature city. As his baby sister bumped into towers and sent blocks tumbling, Nick would yell in slow motion, "*Godzzzzillllla! Nooooo!*"

A few years later, we'd dress up and play *Rambo*. In a photograph of us standing in front of the Christmas tree, Nick has a pair of Mom's nylons tied around his forehead, and I'm wearing a Chicago Bears helmet.

After returning from Oceans Abroad, our relationship reached a deeper level than playtime buddies. Nick and I were four years apart, so when he graduated from high school, I graduated from eighth grade. When I was finishing my senior year, Nick was living in town with some friends. We never really talked about the ship outright, but I think he sensed that something within me had gone out. A flame snuffed. A pool drained. I'd seen it in him four years earlier when a knee injury finished his football career.

Nick had played middle linebacker in high school. Number 45. Even off the field, he walked like Axilles going into battle. Instead of armor, his bronze skin was gilded in tattoos. His hair rippled like the Myrmidon's black sails. His reputation soared beyond golden plains and rocky mountains. Denver was leaving messages, University of Washington mailed brochures, U of O sent athletic shorts.

Third game during his senior year, Nick's team was playing in Missoula. As always, both parents traveled, separately, to the game. I stayed in Helena for a middle school dance. I'd gone to Nick's small fry games when he was in middle school. I'd traveled over two hundred miles to Kalispell and Billings for his high school games. I sat in ninety-degree heat watching his practice scrimmages. The previous weekend, we'd been up in Great Falls clanking cowbells at every tackle. But on this one night, I stayed at a friend's house. No big deal. The next game was home. Then crosstown. Then three more home games. Yet even an eighth grader feels it, that quiet trickle of guilt for having chosen friends over family.

From the painstaking accounts I heard afterward, I constructed the scene in my mind:

The air was crisp, the night charged with cheering fans. The chalk made a perfect grid, ticking each yard to the goal line. Nineteen yards from the opponent's end zone, a black sprinkler head poked out of the grass.

Two minutes to halftime, his team was ahead 28–0. On the field, Nick took his stance, his helmet reflecting the stadium lights. The center snapped the ball, triggering a reaction of cleats and grass. Nick faked right, pivoted left. But something caught his toe.

His knee snapped to the ground.

Dad shot to his feet. Mom clasped her mouth. Trainers rushed onto the field, pointing in outrage at the sprinkler head. Coach Walters put a burly arm around Nick's back and stood him up, his trophy athlete. My brother took two steps, grasped his left knee, and rolled back in the damp grass.

Both parents and all the siblings drove to Butte early Sunday morning, where a family friend opened his imaging center to us. The radiologist clipped the film onto the view box.

Four meniscus tears.

ACL ripped completely in half.

"No. You don't understand. I've gotta play. Can't we just wrap it? He's gotta do something. I've gotta play."

On the car ride back, Dad reached over to him in the front seat. "Don't worry, Nick. It'll be okay. You'll play again."

"Shut up, Dad."

When we got to Dad's house, even Mom came in to help Nick into his bed. He turned his back and stared at the sheetrock wall.

After surgery, visitors rotated through the house like a concession stand at halftime. His football buddies entertained themselves with old-school video games. Coach Walters stopped by before school, at lunch, and after practice. Even coaches from rival teams called to see how he was doing.

But recruiters stopped calling. Letters stopped coming.

The drum beats ceased.

In the years following the injury, I like to think I helped Nick rebuild, as much as a teenager can anyway. We ate Mom's zucchini muffins together and worked out at the fitness club downtown. I drove his truck to get him cans of chew.

He assisted Coach Walters with the next generation of linebackers but eventually stopped attending practice. He invested himself in other trades: electrician work, firefighting, irrigation, landscaping. He liked the satisfaction of envisioning work and then realizing it. He liked working with his hands. But like anyone who's lost his path, he couldn't stick to any one task.

The spring I returned from the ship, I spent a lot of time at Nick's house. I studied for government tests at the kitchen table and ate ground venison his housemate fried up in a cast-iron skillet. I remember talking to Nick outside his house one afternoon. It must've been right before my high school graduation, sometime in late May. I was weighted, feeling the cloud of expectation imposed by small towns. I could hear the murmuring undertones of the community: *What's Jamie Perros going to do now?* I heard it every time someone asked me about my future, about what I'd be majoring in, about where I was going to college. I wondered if they were expecting another fall.

"Everyone's expecting 'great' things," I mumbled to Nick. I couldn't outdo myself, couldn't top sailing the globe. Nor did I want to. I didn't care about setting new goals; I wanted my dream back.

Nick sat down on the porch steps with me. Across the street was a small playground with a lush practice field. I looked at the children climbing the monkey bars and kids on swings pumping the air. When would they learn that life is just a handful of botched plans? Nick's dark eyes roamed the grass. His small fry football practices used to be held on that same field. In red jerseys too big for them, his squad learned about the positions, went over simple plays, and practiced cadence drills. He lived across the street from where his glory days began, yet somehow he had managed to progress, to move past football stats and athletic scholarships. But I couldn't see anything more than the scholarship that had promised me the world.

Nick turned his eyes away from the field and spat. Tobacco juice splattered the sidewalk. "James, life's like a jigsaw puzzle. If one piece doesn't fit, I pick up another one."

"What about the pieces that don't work out?" I searched Nick's face: his rounded nose, his furrowed brow, his dimples that contrasted with his hard outward appearance.

"You toss 'em."

Before I left for the Philippines, Mrs. Lambert had helped me preapprove the credits I would receive from Oceans Abroad so I could graduate from my high school. She assured me that as long as I maintained my 4.0 GPA on the ship, I would be honored as a valedictorian. What she hadn't told me was that there had been talk among the administration about whether or not my name should even appear in the graduation program because, technically, I had decided to leave the school.

When I returned, I completed almost two months' worth of homework I had missed. I read William Faulkner's *As I Lay Dying* in a single night, I wrote response papers in my lined notebook, I memorized American government vocabulary by quizzing myself from homemade flashcards. I caught myself up to the present not out of spite, but because I genuinely enjoyed learning. I actually liked being a student.

I had reached the last week of school. But I still hadn't written my valedictorian speech. I had planned on writing it at a serene beach in Thailand, or while squinting at the Hong Kong skyline. I was supposed to send it to my mother from Asia, who was going to read it at graduation in my stead. If I hadn't returned, would I still have been recognized?

My hard work was tainted.

The day before graduation, I decided to write my speech at Morning Light, a local coffee shop three blocks from Grandstreet. Despite its name, Morning Light was the only coffeehouse in town that stayed open until 10:00 p.m. It's where I went to write high school papers or study for tests, and where my Grandstreet friends and I hung out at lunch breaks during summer theatre camp. In previous semesters, I used to turn off my cell phone and drive to Morning

Light, letting whoever I ran into there shape the course of the night. After returning from the ship, I avoided public places. It was just easier to not talk to people.

Hesitantly, I stepped into Morning Light. My eyes darted from booth to stool to table, dreading the look of familiar faces. It was packed, so of course there were plenty. I ordered the usual, an Irish cream latte, and squeezed into the only empty booth. I stared down at my notebook. Blank lines stared back at me. I began ripping a square napkin one strip at a time.

"Is this seat reserved?"

The voice was playful. I looked up to see my piano teacher's son-in-law, Lio, holding a mug of coffee. He owned an Italian restaurant downtown where my friends and I used to go suiting. "Suiting" involved rummaging through Grandstreet Theatre's costume dungeon, finding outdated yet wearable suit coats and dresses, and then strolling to Aurelio's Ristorante. His younger son and daughter grew up at Grandstreet with me, and his older son had played football with Nick. Something about Lio's family made me gravitate toward them. Their Mediterranean features made me feel as though I was in the company of extended relatives.

Lio sat across from me, his bearded face speckled with silver. "Lio," I said, "I don't know what to do now that Ocea—" I stopped myself. Since returning, I didn't like talking about the ship. "I mean, now that college is approaching. I don't know...what to major in." My future had been consumed by the *Interlude*'s billowing sails. I had thought Oceans Abroad would launch me on a path beyond my wildest dreams. To an international university in Beijing or Christchurch or Athens. I should have looked more closely at theatre-intensive colleges.

Wait. I should have looked at theatre-intensive colleges. I should have strangled my desire to travel. I shouldn't have tried to reach so high. I shouldn't have left my senior class. I shouldn't have listened to the calls of my ancestors. I should have shouldn't have should have shouldn't have have have to have should.

What the hell was I doing in Helena?

Lio set his mug next to my shredded napkin. "You can do whatever you want." He told me that in college, he majored in sociology. After he graduated, he was a police officer, then a restaurateur, and now a youth pastor. He explained how each role complemented the next, but that he hadn't set out to do just one thing in life. "My major didn't dictate what I became. And I certainly didn't plan on playing all these different roles, but I've gotten to." A smile peeked through his beard before he took a last gulp of coffee.

I peered into my latte, trying to connect his story to my own. Maybe it was okay that I was back. Maybe it was okay if life didn't go as planned.

Maybe.

As quickly as he appeared, Lio was gone. I looked at the seat he'd occupied just moments ago. He had bussed his mug, but a single napkin was left at his spot. I clicked my pen, slid the napkin over to my side, and started writing.

The morning of graduation, Mom called from the bottom of the stairs: "Want me to iron anything?"

"No," I called down. "The robe will cover everything up, anyway."

"But don't you want to know that you look nice underneath?"

"I don't care." I picked out an orange t-shirt, a plaid skirt, and flip flops.

A few hours later, I got out of my car and walked onto the football field, where graduations were normally held. The sky was bright blue, not a cloud in sight.

We were an overachieving class; fifteen students had maintained straight A's throughout high school. Most of the valedictorians gave humorous speeches. One referenced Shorty, the hot derby horse of 2004. There might've been a couple references from *The Lord of the Rings*. And then it was my turn.

I stepped up to the podium. Rows and rows of seats lined the football field. The Montana sun reflected on the metal stadium. In the distance, mountains rose behind the stands. I didn't feel nervous, just out of place. These were my peers, the people I'd gone to school with for four years. Some I even knew from preschool. My robe swished as I propped my arms on the podium. The heat made my cotton shirt stick to my back. I unfolded the napkin crease by crease. I had finally been inspired, and even now, I wasn't going to throw away an opportunity to perform. I began as I would a monologue, pausing for effect and lingering on double meaning.

"Life is unpredictable." My voice sounded strange in the microphone. It echoed across the grass and up into the stadium. "You may slip on your sandals, thinking they'll be perfect for the occasion, but find that you should've worn crushed velvet stilettos. You may pull on leather boots, when you very well should have worn suede. Or you may discover that the soles of your lucky basketball shoes finally fell apart. You may want to wear your '*killer boots, man!*'—and you can—but know that you can get to where you want to go without them. It may hurt more, it may not be as glamorous, but know that you can do it without the luck, without the planning, without the varnish. Life is spontaneous. So jump in barefoot."

I kicked off my flip flops and brandished them over my head. Applause broke out, accompanied by cowbells and a few catcalls. I figured the *WOOOO!*'s were from those like Nick who caught that I'd just referenced *Dumb and Dumber* in a valedictorian speech.

Ah, yes, the poetic justice of an eighteen-year-old.

The summer after graduating from high school, I performed in the musical *Barnum*, my last production at Grandstreet Theatre. "Your body is the greatest instrument you have," our director, Brooke, told us the first morning of rehearsals. "This summer theatre conservatory will push it to the limit. You will be treated as professional actors, with rehearsals twelve hours a day. Acting class in the morning, music and choreography in the afternoon, and run-throughs every night for the next month."

She flicked her feathery hair behind her shoulders. Her petite build betrayed not the slightest hint of weakness. Her stance was firm. Her sculpted arms relaxed at her sides. Brooke, an alumnus of Grandstreet Theatre, had just graduated from a prestigious, cutthroat theatre conservatory. She had returned to her hometown to direct *Barnum*. Brooke's formative years occurred on the same stage where we adolescent aspirants now sat. Her words struck notes of wisdom, of expertise, of triumphs we longed for and of mastery we sought.

Set in the mid-1800s, the musical traced the eccentric life of Phineas Taylor Barnum and his career with sideshows and circuses. With juggling clowns, a Ferris wheel, and a trapeze, the show was a spectacle when fully staged and choreographed. I was cast as Chairy, the female lead and P. T. Barnum's pragmatic wife. While Barnum was a dreamer with a flair for "humbugging," Chairy was a no-nonsense, headstrong woman who wanted her husband to settle down into a respectable profession.

Onstage, I couldn't get into my character. I struggled with everything, from Chairy's motives to her blocking. Each morning, I had script sessions with Brooke and the actor who played Barnum. I wrote pages and pages of notes about Chairy's personality and designed an extensive character profile. I analyzed each scene and wrote out the objectives and subtext for each line. But for some reason, I was unable to emotionally connect to my character. In the scene where Chairy encourages Barnum to believe in his dreams, I couldn't feel her optimism. In the scene where she discovers he's having an affair with a famous opera singer, I couldn't feel her torment. In the scene where Chairy welcomes Barnum home, I couldn't channel what must've been coursing through her heart.

During rehearsal one night, Brooke shouted at me from the second row: "Feel!" I caught glimpses of her jotting notes on her dreaded clipboard. No doubt I'd receive a diatribe regarding my flatness, my inexpressiveness, and my lack of compassion toward my dear husband.

In a later scene, I was interrupted again on a platform resembling part of a circus tent. "Chairy!" Brooke yelled from the house. "Stop acting with your forehead!"

"What?"

Nimbly, Brooke jumped onstage and looked up at me. "Use your words, your heart to convey emotion."

I blinked down at her.

"Your forehead. Don't wrinkle it."

After ruminating on that note, I realized that I was engaging in physical acting—manipulating my body to look as though I was feeling something. I raised my eyebrows for excitement, up-turned my lips for happiness, threw my hands up for delight. But I didn't feel any of these emotions.

A year later, I would learn why I was experiencing this numbing phenomenon, which had everything to do with the ship. But at the time, I had no answers. To me, my performance in *Barnum* was quickly becoming another failure in my teenage life. Too contrived. Too forced.

The only peace I felt was during the five minutes before rehearsals. Every afternoon, one of the cast members played the same song from the sound booth as we stretched onstage. The Hawaiian singer Israel Kamakawiwoʻole's "Somewhere Over the Rainbow" drifted through the empty house. I loved the meditative, communal ritual of our cast quietly warming up together.

Only to be replaced with more disconnection.

Every night after rehearsal, I drove myself home and wrote into my journal: *What the hell is my problem? I'm so frustrated up there. I can't connect to anything.* While the rest of the cast bonded, went to the park after rehearsals, and watched the summer Olympics, I holed up in my bedroom and smoldered into my journal: *I'm the female lead and I can't even juggle. Everyone else can juggle. This is ridiculous.*

During dinner break one evening, I drove one of the younger cast members, Owen, to his house, where we helped ourselves to leftovers. As I scooped spaghetti onto our plates, I checked a voice message on my cell phone. Halfway through, I stopped dishing up the food.

"Who is it?" Owen asked.

"I don't know. A guy. With girls laughing in the background."

Owen was sitting at the countertop. He reached his hand out for my cell phone and listened to the message. "Well, this is messed up," he said.

"I know, right?"

"Does he sound familiar?"

"Not really, but the laughing kind of sounds like one of my friends."

The voice message had been left by an angry, drunk-sounding male. Between the *bitch*'s and *bullshit*'s, Owen and I pieced the message together. The male was criticizing me for spending so much time at Grandstreet. He called me *high and mighty* and *too good for us*. I concluded that the *us* were my friends from high school.

"I don't even have time to see my own mother," I told Owen, "let alone anyone else." With opening night approaching, *Barnum* rehearsals continued to fill mornings, afternoons, evenings, and nights. I tried to shrug off the message, but the angry voice and laughter taunted me the rest of the week.

When *Barnum* opened, few friends came to see the show. My family, however, attended multiple performances. Nick enjoyed it so much he asked if I could find him one of our production t-shirts, but none were large enough to fit his ex-linebacker build.

The musical was received well by the community. No one seemed to notice a difference in my quality of acting. I sang the right notes. I completed the correct steps in my choreography. I delivered my lines exactly as they had been written in the script. But I went through the motions on autopilot, unable to access a full range of emotions. What had been second nature to me since I was nine was turning into an indecipherable language.

The stage no longer felt like home.

BETA

Complications:
the alignment of
opposing forces against one another

III

How awful to be attached to a place.

~Aristofanes, *Wasps*

My new voice instructor, Cindy, scrutinized my 8x10 resume and black-and-white headshot. Threads of silver gathered at her temples, gleaming in the August sunlight. She reminded me of an older version of Maria from *West Side Story*. Peering up at me from her grand piano, she pursed her red lips, then looked back down. Either she liked what she saw, or she thought us an incompatible match. "What are you doing here?" she asked. Her voice was soft, pleasant like Maria's.

"I'm here for my voice lesson," I said, stepping up to the music stand.

"Yes, but what are you doing *here*?"

I knew what she meant the first time. It's what I'd been asking myself since the day I stepped onto this spongy campus in the Pacific Northwest. Despite my years of musical theatre training at Grandstreet, I had chosen a college that had virtually no musical theatre or dance programs. In the wake of preparing for Oceans Abroad, applying to college had been pushed aside. As a formality, I had applied to two universities the fall of my senior year. Before I embarked, I hurriedly accepted the one in Oregon.

Since the drug reaction to Lariam, I found myself on a path for which I hadn't planned. I hadn't auditioned for conservatories like other seniors at Grandstreet. I hadn't even researched this college's theatre department. Despite the challenges I experienced in *Barnum*, the only subject I considered majoring in—the only thing that made me feel a sense of purpose—was theatre. I enrolled in an acting class but didn't think the department was a good fit. The plays they produced were graphic, disturbing works, with jarring machine gun sound effects or watching a man give birth onstage.

"Well," I responded to my new voice instructor, "I want to continue studying musical theatre." I was relieved to see that her bookcase was stocked with collections of Bernstein and Sondheim, Ira and George Gershwin, Stephen Schwartz, and even Jason Robert Brown.

"You've got the right person for the job," she said.

Her office smelled of cinnamon and orange spice. In the corner, a loveseat was draped with green and purple blankets. A wool pillow with the silhouette of an elephant sat cockeyed on it. I wanted to straighten the pillow. I wanted to run my hand over the blankets, to stretch myself out on that sofa and impart to Cindy my confusion about the future, my thoughts of transferring to a performing arts school, and the tension I'd been feeling in my jaw since starting college.

By the third voice lesson, I did just that.

"I feel anxious. All the time." I closed *Sondheim: Female Solos* on the music stand in front of me. Cindy stayed at the piano bench but gestured for me to sit on the loveseat. "I don't know what's wrong with me," I continued. "I wake up every morning with my jaw clenched. That's why these vocal warm-ups you gave me are so helpful. "

She nodded, a look of motherly concern on her face. She wore thick mascara and blush, perhaps an old musical theatre habit. "And you've been researching other schools?"

"Yes. I've narrowed it down to two. A conservatory in Chicago, or a university in California. Except I had a dream last night that made me nervous about the one in Chicago. I woke up sweating." I petted the felt elephant. "Going to a conservatory, with no option of majoring in something academic too, doesn't sit right with me. The California school seems like a safer option. It's a full college, so I could double major in theatre and something 'practical.'"

Cindy smiled. "Sounds like you're on the right track."

I think she felt satisfaction from cultivating artists too free to fit the confines of the music department. I pieced together that Cindy, a new professor, was given students who were not classically trained. Essentially, she was assigned to "inferior" freshmen who resisted filling the mold of an opera singer. The music department was not concerned with belting, had no time for "monologuing lyrics," couldn't be bothered with choreographing a song. Cindy, with her own impressive musical theatre resume, was therefore labeled inferior too.

I found other aspects of the university confining. The college reminded me of living in a small town. I hadn't realized that the undergraduate population was under 2,000 students, slightly larger than my high school had been. A few years later, I would be thankful for the small size and familiar faces and surroundings, but during my freshman year, the school reminded me too much of Helena. I was afraid that if one person found out I had failed to complete my program abroad, then the news would be heard around the campus, echoing what happened a handful of months earlier.

The campus in Oregon was situated around a grassy quad, each side framed by brick buildings and leaved trees. A few blocks away, I discovered a circular monument of the world's flags. In the rain, I liked to stand in the middle of the circle and try to identify the flags from the countries I was supposed to have seen on Oceans Abroad. Maybe it was a kind of torture, but being surrounded by all those flags made me forget, briefly, that I hadn't sailed the world.

I lived in a faded brick building with high ceilings and tall windows. Samantha, a friend of mine from high school choir, also attended the college. She and I had sung in the alto section and shared an affinity for fantasy films and Legolas posters. She lived on the first floor with a roommate from Wyoming. My dorm was in the basement. The basement had low ceilings, small windows, and heavy doors that slammed shut. Something about being down there made me uneasy, so I usually hung out upstairs in the girls' room. We befriended a few sophomore guys and got on a *Moulin Rouge!* kick fall semester. When we weren't watching the film, we were listening to the soundtrack. Samantha competed with the boys' room for who had the loudest speakers. We never considered that not everybody on the first floor was obsessed with Baz Luhrmann show tunes.

I found being in a new place where people didn't know about my past refreshing. But there's a fine line between privacy and secrecy. I kept Oceans Abroad secret, and in such secrecy, it festered in the darkness. Samantha never mentioned it either. Sometimes in her room I referenced it briefly, usually as a division between time periods—the before, a void, the after. What I didn't realize was that the more I suppressed what had happened, the more the experience manifested itself through my body.

A few months into fall semester, I went to my weekly voice lesson as usual. "Let's try that run again," Cindy instructed from the piano.

I sang two octaves.

"Make sure you use your diaphragm," she said, touching her belly to demonstrate.

I sang two more octaves.

"You don't sound right," Cindy said. "Are you feeling okay?"

I tugged my yellow sweater. "I don't know," I said. "I haven't been feeling well."

"I can hear it in your voice."

I cringed at the complete transparency of being a performing artist. To a fine-tuned instructor, the voice betrays all. Just drank a caffeinated beverage? They'll hear hoarseness in your larynx. Just ate ice cream? They'll detect phlegm rattling in your throat. Just smoked a cigarette? Don't even bother showing up to your lesson.

"Did you stay up late last night? Working on a paper? Studying?"

"No." My cheeks began to burn.

She gestured to the loveseat.

Sitting, I massaged my jaw muscles. I'd been so fatigued the last few weeks that I could've slept right there on the sofa. "I feel like I'm falling apart. My stomach hurts. And my throat is burning"—I pointed to the base of my neck—"right here. And I've been having, like, constant diarrhea. Sorry," I added embarrassedly.

She didn't flinch. "Have you made an appointment at the health center on campus?"

I stopped massaging my jaw. "Should I?"

Her hair bounced in a single nod. "Let's call it quits for today," she said, closing her songbook. "Go back to your dorm and rest." Her eyes flickered in the weak November sunlight. "We need you sounding strong for your audition in California."

I didn't make an appointment at the health center. Instead, I timed myself delivering my monologue. The entire scholarship audition for the school in California had to be under three minutes. Get in, show your range, get out. I'd done many auditions like this at Grandstreet and had carefully chosen my pieces: "I'm Not Afraid of Anything" from Jason Robert Brown's *Songs for a New World*, and a monologue from Lee Blessing's *Independence*.

As the weeks passed, I continued practicing my audition and revising my application essay, never letting my schoolwork slip behind. I found that college offered massive amounts of free time. My roommate was gone a lot because she was on the swim team, so I memorized at leisure, designating her desk as the pretend adjudicators. But I missed my practice space in the living room back home. I hadn't cried since April, when Ifigeneia's grief helped me indirectly express my own.

In college, I didn't think I deserved to cry. I had to be tough. I had to prove that I wasn't weak. I had to hide my shortfalls, hide my disappointment in myself. Going to the gym helped me drive away feelings of physical inadequacy. My body, I believed, was the reason why I had to leave the ship. *No one else was so seasick that they couldn't walk on deck without puking. No one else reacted so severely to an antimalarial that they had to be sent home. Everyone else had been able to thrive at sea. Everyone else had been able to stomach antimalarials.* To mute these repetitive thoughts, I exercised. In the corner of the cardio area, I stepped onto a treadmill and blared hip-hop music into my head. All I wanted to hear was the bass pounding in my chest and the soles of my shoes hitting the track. I worked out sometimes twice a day, six to seven times a week.

Christmas break was approaching and the dorms were clearing out. My roommate had already left, traveling north to Seattle. I still had one more exam, so I spent the last few days studying verb conjugations, *por* versus *para*, and vocabulary related to *la hacienda*. The morning of my Spanish exam, I woke up early to a dull burning in my ribcage. I couldn't fall back asleep, so I stacked vocabulary flashcards on my paisley comforter, ready to quiz myself. As I rotated through each card, the burning intensified. Suddenly, my right side seized with pain.

The neat stack of flashcards scattered across the bedspread.

Racking my brain, I tried to recall what I'd eaten yesterday. Pizza? Pasta? Late night cereal? I couldn't remember. Like fire, the pain blazed up through my stomach and down to my belly button. My cell phone lay on my desk. When Cindy suggested I visit the health center on campus, I had entered the phone number into my contact list, but done little else.

"Hello," I said desperately into the phone. "I'm in pain."

The receptionist asked a series of questions.

"My stomach. Well, my side. On the right. When I woke up."

She asked if I could walk to the health center on my own.

Rain smeared the windowpane. My stomach spasmed. "No."

Five minutes later, a dispatcher arrived at my dorm building, not in a car, but in a golf cart. The driver had a white beard, like Santa Claus wearing a black getup. He drove me, in the wind and rain, through the quad.

At the health center, I went directly into a patient room. The nurse practitioner asked me what I'd last eaten, when I had my last bowel movement, how I slept last night, and on a scale of one to ten,

"How would you rate your pain?"

"Eleven."

Reluctantly, I let her touch my abdomen. She determined that I had some type of gastritis, or inflammation of the stomach lining. She gave me a GI cocktail and made me wait on the crunchy exam table until it took effect. The thick liquid numbed my tongue and throat. Twenty minutes later she came back in and asked, "How would you rate your pain?"

"Ten."

She examined my stomach again, asked me to describe my daily bowel patterns, left me in the room for a while, then returned carrying a paper bag filled with medicine. "This is a liquid antacid. It should help with the burning sensation. And here's a seven-day sample of a proton pump inhibitor. It will help manage the acid in your stomach." Nothing she gave me addressed the pain in my right side, the epicenter of my attack. She tentatively diagnosed me with irritable bowel syndrome. IBS, as the disorder is commonly called, is the occurrence of unpredictable constipation and diarrhea.

Eventually, the pain subsided enough for me to return to my dorm. My side gnawed dully, but the thought of having to reschedule a final exam pushed it to the back of my mind. My Spanish test was in an hour. When I got back to my room, Samantha came down to check on me. "I'm right upstairs," she said. "If you need anything, lemme know." Half an hour later, we trudged through the rain together to take our respective exams. I realized I was still in my pajama bottoms. "Ah, who cares," she said, waving her hand. This marked the beginning of Samantha's long-term care for me in college.

During Christmas break, I flew to California for the theatre scholarship audition. I would finish spring semester in Oregon, and if all went as planned, I'd begin my theatre training in California fall quarter.

The theatre department at the university in California reminded me of Grandstreet. Their season of plays honored classic American playwrights, as well as Shakespeare. They even produced a spring musical in conjunction with the dance and music departments. I'd never seen anything like it: all three departments collaborating. The theatre and dance programs were wedded, which meant students could participate in both main stage plays and dance concerts because performance schedules did not conflict. Many other colleges did not sync their performance calendars. Students had to choose which department to remain loyal to, which talent to hone while neglecting the others.

With Cindy's vocal instruction to guide me through my song and years of acting lessons from Grandstreet, I entered the audition confidently, feeling the stage floor firmly beneath my character shoes. I introduced myself to the adjudicators, looking each one in the eye as Charlotte had taught me at theatre school. I started with my monologue, and ended the audition with my song. Imagining Jason Robert Brown himself was accompanying me, I sang a brassy version of "I'm Not Afraid of Anything."

A few months later, I received an acceptance letter from the college and a scholarship offer from the theatre department. Feeling that old sense of excitement, I tried to squelch it. What if something happened? What if I was setting myself up for another disappointment? Another botched dream? I tried not to romanticize the school in California as I had Oceans Abroad, but I couldn't help feeling that I was on the right path once more, one that could feed my soul and satisfy the performer within me.

My digestive tract, however, was performing worse each day.

I ate yogurt: Diarrhea.

Cheese: Constipation.

So I cut dairy out of my diet.

I ate flour tortillas: Diarrhea.

Bagels: Constipation.

So I cut out wheat.

Soup made my intestines squeeze.

Carbonated beverages gave me acid reflux.

Raw vegetables produced gas.

I didn't know what to do, so I tried to ignore my symptoms and pretend I felt fine. I exercised more, and I found a ballet studio downtown. I thought ballet lessons would be an effective way to prime myself for the theatre program in California.

One night in March, Samantha's roommate, Ruby, found me sitting on the wet concrete steps outside our dorm building. Tucking her auburn braid into her hood, Ruby sat down next to me. "You look exhausted," she said.

"I am." I'd just walked back from ballet. My tights sank deep into my stomach. The leotard straps cut into my shoulders. My feet were stuffed into rain boots, ballet slippers and all.

"You're not a ballerina, right?" Ruby asked.

"No. It's not my favorite dance form."

"Then why don't you stop going?"

"It's helping my dance technique," I said.

"We both know your body has withstood enough abuse."

That word—abuse—struck a note of truth I had been refusing to hear since starting college. Hanging my head, I cried into Ruby's jacket.

Looking back, I see how perceptive Ruby was, how she named so directly what I refused to acknowledge. My behavior toward myself was just that: self-defeating emotional abuse, and self-punishing physical abuse. What I remember most about my freshman year of college is being the last one on the treadmill at the gym, cramming yoga and cardio into my schedule, denying my body rest because I believed it had betrayed me on the ship. An "adverse drug reaction" meant nothing to me. I didn't understand antimalarials. All I understood was my body being too weak to adapt to life at sea. Why couldn't I partake in the adventure of a lifetime? Why couldn't I soar the way my soul yearned to? Because my greatest instrument had failed me.

Eight years later, when I was in graduate school, I came across a short story I wrote my freshman year of college. I had comically named the piece "The Colon Speaks." All of the details in the story, aside from my colon verbally speaking to me, were true: the days of constipation followed by streaming diarrhea, the rawness around my anus from wiping so much, the heartburn and intestinal cramping.

I read the story to my boyfriend, Luke, a medical student. We were renting an apartment near Wayland Square in Providence, Rhode Island. Luke was born and raised in Montana, too, and grew up performing at his own local community theatre. He had blue eyes, freckles, and the build of an ex-defensive end. Colleges in Montana had offered him football scholarships, but he declined the Montana dream to study pre-med on the East Coast.

In middle school, Luke and I had met at Grandstreet's summer theatre camp. He was an exotic out-of-towner, so naturally, he became a heartthrob to us locals. Whenever I retell our story, Luke often takes over, and describes how he became enchanted by a beautiful young woman. "I was thirteen," I'll counter, "with a nose too big for me, acne, and eyebrows I hadn't learned how to pluck." We had an awkward pre-teen crush at best.

In high school, Luke returned to theatre camp. That summer, I was performing in *Once on This Island*. After attending one of the shows, he drove me home, where we kissed in the driveway at my mom's house. We kept in touch during college, but our calls became infrequent. Then in 2010, our paths finally began to converge. We met up in Portland, Oregon, for our twenty-fifth birthdays, which fell three days apart. I took him out for shots of ouzo at Alexis Greek Restaurant on Burnside, and then to Voodoo Doughnuts. We ordered a bag of their wild creations and found a bench at a riverfront park nearby. That night, with peanut butter and chocolate glaze oozing down my fingers, I kept seeing the word LONGEVITY in my mind. Shortly after, I started looking at graduate programs in New England, and moved to Providence half a year later.

Luke told me that from a medical viewpoint, "The Colon Speaks" sounded like a classic case of irritable bowel syndrome. From a humanistic perspective, he said that the humor in the piece was indicative of something much greater. "It seems as though you needed to tell the story this way. To use humor to approach the subject matter."

"Well, I was writing about taking dumps." I tried to lighten the mood, but knew Luke's words were true. The story alluded to something other than my bowel patterns, something Ruby described as my "incredible routine of punishment."

Ruby and I have remained close. Her penchant for history led her to a PhD program in Cambridge. My graduate school was in Boston, so I often spent the night at her apartment to lessen my commutes from Providence to Boston and back. One afternoon, I sat down with her to dredge up the memories of our freshman year in Oregon. But I was distracted by some photos above her kitchen table.

"You're the hottest Ewok I've ever seen," I said.

"Oh, yeah. That was from Comic-Con in San Diego." In the photos, Ruby was wearing a fuzzy brown suit and a hood with round ears. Draped over her head was a tattered orange cloak resembling the tribal attire of George Lucas's Ewoks. "I wore that costume to class on Halloween this year. When I was crossing the street, this guy yelled out of his taxi, "Ey! Ew an Ewok?' It was the greatest day of my life."

We tried to perfect our imitations of Boston's dialect. Being from the Old West, we were used to hearing double negatives, dropped g's and long a's, ain't's and gonna's instead of the nasal concoction of English we'd grown accustomed to in New England.

Our laughter dissolved as Ruby shared her memories of my nineteen-year-old self. "I remember the slow progression," she said, "of finding out what happened on the boat. Bits and pieces. It was a long time until you told the story about having to go home. When you did tell me, it really seemed as if it had happened a month ago. Like there was no lapse in time."

She poured us glasses of iced tea, just as she used to in college. "I really sympathized with you," she continued, "because we share the same personality. I understand that dream of building up to something, of putting so much pressure on yourself to succeed. I swear I never saw you in real clothes freshman year. You were always in workout shorts. I always ran into you when you were coming to or from the gym. I remember how much praise you got as you were getting thinner. Thinness is actually a sign of ill health. But because it's socially praised, no one gets it checked out." She told me that she was studying for a field exam in a subject called anthropology of the body. "The social benefits of being thin," she explained, "mask any underlying problems associated with weight loss."

Ruby set her pink cup onto the table. "The most vivid memory I have of us freshman year is when I was starting to get a cold fall semester, and you told me to exercise."

"Oh, no." I laughed darkly. "I remember that."

"'Yeah,' you said, 'whenever I get sick, I go to the gym to sweat it out.' When our friends told me to stop exercising because—you know—I was just getting worse, I said, 'No. Jamie told me to exercise the sickness out of me.'"

I shook my head. My nineteen-year-old self was the last person from whom she should've sought medical advice.

Ruby continued, "I always thought you were very...mean to yourself. I was like that too, but toward my schoolwork. Your hardness was more directed at your body. You didn't strike me as someone indulgent. I read romance novels and watched *The Lord of the Rings* in my spare time. You were routinized, driven. What struck me most was an incongruity between the way you treated yourself and the way you treated others. You were caring and spiritual—you were very kind to people."

I looked into my empty cup. "Just not to myself."

Γ

Oh, light! Let me beseech you.

~Euripides, *Hekebe*

I got my driver's license the summer I turned sixteen, which was also the summer of *Once on This Island*, when I discovered Oceans Abroad. On the day of the driving test, I held the steering wheel at "ten o'clock" and "two o'clock" and remembered a friend's advice to drive slowly over the railroad tracks. Other than parallel parking, the test was a breeze. The photo on my driver's license captured me in my summer prime: blue halter top, unwashed curls starting to dread, and a look of utter triumph.

My first car was an old stick shift. On Saturday afternoons, Dad took me and my little brother to the VA hospital where he worked. A residential area framed the back of the grounds where VA doctors lived with their families. It was a quiet neighborhood with wide roads on level ground. Dad thought it'd be the perfect place for me to practice driving.

At a stop sign, I stalled the car four times in a row. From the corner of my eye, I could see a pack of kids on bicycles gathering at the street corner. In the backseat, belly giggles were erupting from Johnny. I took a breath and tried one more time to release the brake while simultaneously easing the gas. I knew in theory how the pedal exchange was supposed to work—Dad kept pantomiming it with his hands—but it never translated to my feet. *How can I dance in musicals,* I thought, *but not get this stupid step?*

The car lurched again.

"They're pointing at you!" Dad said.

Sure enough, the kids were pointing and laughing at our balking car. Feeling my frustration rising—being unable to master an exchange of clutch and gas, being so close to finally getting a car but being unable to drive it, being laughed at by children—made me want to burst into swear words. Luckily, my frustration gave way to laughter.

"Maybe," Johnny giggled, "you should ask to trade with that kid's trike."

Instead, we traded in the car for a '91 hatchback nicknamed Goldie—with automatic transmission. Goldie got me everywhere, and the trunk quickly turned into an extra closet for my character shoes, dance tights, swim suits, and gym shorts. My Grandstreet friends and I spent countless winter and summer nights in Goldie, blasting musicals after rehearsals.

After my freshman year of college, Goldie carried no passengers. No music, just my cussing outbursts after being told from doctors that nothing was wrong with me. The frustration of trying to conquer stick shift was nothing compared to the anger of being conquered by inexplicable, invalidated symptoms.

Since the abdominal attack in my dorm room before Christmas break in Oregon, another sent me to the ER in June during a family reunion in Duluth. When we got back to Helena, I underwent an upper endoscopy. The test revealed a hiatal hernia. "Most people have hiatal hernias without ever knowing it," the gastroenterologist said. "They're very common."

The GI specialist treated my hiatal hernia as an insignificant finding. I fell into none of the common risk factors: I wasn't a smoker, wasn't overweight, wasn't over the age of fifty. What I heard when the doctor told me how common hiatal hernias are was this: your esophagus is not burning, your chest is not burning, you have a barely perceptible hiatal hernia just like everybody else. What I wanted to say, but didn't, was that I don't want to be compared to everybody else. I care about being looked at as an individual with my own unique chemistry and makeup, with my own history. Study my case. Don't compare it to what "should be" common symptoms and then declare you must be fine, it's in your head, relieve your stress, take a break, relax. What if my hiatal hernia was causing my symptoms?

Years later, I would learn that violent, repeated vomiting can cause a hiatal hernia.

In June, my primary care physician ordered abdominal and pelvic ultrasounds, which identified no cause for my raging gastrointestinal tract.

In July, a GI specialist ordered an MR cholangiography, which detected free fluid and a possible filling defect in my liver. In other words, it was possible that my liver had a blood clot. I felt a little scared at the sound of these findings, but all I really wanted was an answer to my abdominal pain.

In August, the GI specialist ordered a Doppler ultrasound to follow up on the possible filling defect. I drove to the hospital in Helena. During the Doppler ultrasound, cool gel was squirted onto my belly and a plastic device slowly circled my skin. After the procedure, I walked out to the hospital parking lot. Goldie was waiting for me, my faithful chariot. I tucked my skirt underneath my thighs and rested in the driver's seat. I didn't have the will to turn the key in the ignition. My hands rested on the steering wheel—fuchsia nail polish wearing off, stripped like flames. The steering wheel should've felt hot; Goldie had been in the parking lot for over an hour. But I couldn't feel the August heat. Only the squeezing of my intestines, only the burning of my esophagus. Only the fear of having another attack.

"You look like a model!" a family friend had said last week at the mall. "I saw you walking down the aisle and thought, *How slender, how graceful, how thin!*" My thighs bowed outward like a wishbone, and my knee joints looked like rawhide knots. *I shouldn't be this thin*, I had wanted to retort. *No one should be this thin.* I hadn't exercised since returning home for summer break, but still I had continued to lose weight. I'd abandoned my regimented workout schedule because my bowels were in too much pain to exercise, even for me. The pain gave way to feelings of helplessness. Helplessness was giving way to anger.

An unopened envelope from the university in California was jammed into the passenger seat. I was supposed to start fall quarter in September, but I'd just applied for a deferral for "medical reasons," reasons that hadn't been identified by my primary care physician, GI specialist, or ER doctors. I jerked the envelope from the passenger seat and threw it at the window. "I hate this shit!"

Goldie kept my voice safe inside, unheard by the external world of calm facade. I maintained an impassive expression on my face despite the storms that roiled beneath. I hated the rudeness from receptionists, hated feeling as if I had to prove myself worthy of the fifteen minutes for which I'd be penciled in. Aside from annual checkups, I had never needed to visit doctors before the ship. I never had stomach problems or bowel problems or any long-term health concerns until I returned. I should've been performing with a summer stock theatre company, getting primed for my studies in California. Yet here I was, holed up in my car, in my hometown, grasping at answers for why I was taking a medical leave in the fall. I thought about the Doppler ultrasound and whether it would reveal the source of my symptoms. A car drove by. A voice of doubt gained volume. What if the medical tests were right and there was nothing wrong with me? What if my symptoms were all in my head? What if I'd been causing my own deterioration this entire time?

I wanted to scream. Instead, I pounded the horn: EEEEEEEEEE. Startled birds flew from a nearby tree. My palm continued to press the horn, creating a frequency that cleared my head of anger for one golden moment. Not knowing where to go, I started the ignition and shifted into reverse.

When I interviewed my mother in the fall of 2012, I asked her about the summer of flames, as I've come to think of this period. "It was a sad time," she recalled, "a quiet time. A delicate time. Too many unknowns, too many things happening to your body. With no answers. It was scary for us, especially when you went to the ER in Duluth and you were vomiting blood. You told me one day—you said, 'I feel like I'm dying inside.' But you couldn't just watch yourself fade. You had to do something. You wanted to be in another part of the world, with Marika. What she represented to you. The traveler."

My sister was back in Leipzig with old college friends, traveling and learning the German language. Mom and I combined our airline points to buy a ticket. I flew to Germany at the end of July and stayed with Marika for two weeks. The countryside was so green. I remember having an epic bowel movement from the sausage and heavy dairy, and then I didn't poop for eight days, until I returned to Helena.

The day I got back, Mom picked me up from the airport and took me home. The next morning, I was sitting at the kitchen table eating a bowl of cereal when my intestines writhed back to life. The bathroom was just off the kitchen, so I made it in time. After the first hard stool passed, the rest of my fecal matter streamed out like liquid.

From the kitchen, Mom heard gasps coming from the bathroom. She knocked gently on the door, asking if I was okay. I apologized for the smell and told her she could come in. "You had tears squeezing out the corners of your eyes," she said.

We climbed into her car and headed to the emergency room. On the way, I told her I couldn't hold it. Owen's house was close by, so we detoured there. His older brother answered the door. Mom explained that I needed to use the bathroom. I remember his concerned, slightly confused face, and then I remember their frilly pink bathroom with no air freshener spray. Diarrhea surged through my anus. My hands clamped my t-shirt, praying for an end to the pain.

At the hospital's ER, a physician walked into my exam room. He told me that my past lab history indicated elevated amylase and lipase levels, enzymes produced by the pancreas.

"I know."

"And Dr. Pitney knew you had pancreatitis?"

"Yeah."

"And she still said you could travel internationally? With this, and your GI history?"

"I asked her specifically, before getting the ticket. She said she saw no reason why it would be a problem for me to travel abroad."

The doctor didn't respond, but a shake of his head said everything.

In the end, I was discharged as I had been in Oregon and Minnesota, with no conclusive diagnosis but irritable bowel syndrome. Take fiber two to three times a day. Stick to a BRAT diet of bananas, rice, applesauce, and toast.

The slew of medical appointments I had that summer of 2005 instigated frustration. And anger. And rage. Attempting to remember more, in the fall of 2012 I tracked down my medical records and had them sent to my apartment in Providence. As I turned each page, my hands shook. Reading about myself felt strange. The medical notes were intimate yet depersonalized, written by people I barely knew. Toward the bottom of the stack, I came to the last appointment with my primary care physician, dated 8/16/2005. I didn't need medical records to remember that visit. It was just after going to the ER in Helena, and just before the Doppler ultrasound.

Judith Pitney was the primary care physician I had been seeing since returning from the ship. When I began working with her to identify the cause of my gastrointestinal symptoms, I remember how hopeful I felt about aligning myself with a doctor who was a woman. She would listen. She would understand the plight of women, how, so often, we're told that our symptoms are all in our head.

At our last appointment together, I remember lying on the exam table while she percussed the four quadrants of my abdomen. "Everything sounds fine," she said, removing the stethoscope from her ears.

"Then why am I hurting?"

"Describe the pain to me again." Her request seemed twofold; I suspected that she half-wanted to solve this GI anomaly before her, and half-wanted to dismiss me so she could focus on patients with more concrete complaints.

"My esophagus is burning," I explained for what seemed like the fiftieth time. "And I still feel like I'm going to pass out before bowel movements. I can't do anything I used to—I don't know what to do."

Dr. Pitney looked at my chart. "The medication I prescribed should be promoting regular bowel movements."

"I read that drug label," I said, "and noticed that side effects include constipation and diarrhea—which is what we're trying to treat in the first place."

Her eyes narrowed. "That's why I've also prescribed fiber. Are you taking it?"

"Yes."

I used to wonder what I looked like through Dr. Pitney's eyes. I imagine she saw an immature, postadolescent teen. When I reported symptoms, all I needed to hear was an acknowledgement of my pain, a simple "oh, that must be frustrating" phrase of compassion.

Unfortunately, symptom reporting is not a straightforward process for either the patient or the physician. It's as if the doctor is expected to see an entire house by peeking through a keyhole. The patient, from her own perspective, feels like she is throwing open every door and window in the house and is baffled by the doctor's inability to see inside. Yet there's more than one process at work when presenting physical complaints. American psychologist Dr. James Pennebaker describes symptom reporting as "a strategy to elicit help from others." When these indirect cries are not heard, the patient can feel invalidated.

When the experience of physical symptoms *is* acknowledged, a patient's health can improve. European psychologists Dr. Zoe Chouliara and Dr. Thanos Karatzias believe that explanations provided to patients "can facilitate coping and resilience." However, if symptoms are not acknowledged, then their health can actually worsen. Chouliara and Karatzias conclude that a doctor's "failure to manage physical symptoms effectively will result in high levels of distress for both the patient and the physician." This research makes perfect sense in hindsight, but at the time, my sight was as limited as my physician's.

At the end of our appointment, Dr. Pitney was standing in the center of the room. I was sitting on the exam table, legs crossed like linked chain mail. Frustrated, I let out a long sigh.

"Jamie," Dr. Pitney said, looking directly at me. "You are what we would call a hypochondriac." Before I could speak, defend myself, she continued, "I'll refer you to a therapist." Her eyes scanned my thin forearms and protruding collarbone. "And a nutritionist."

I was outraged by what her words insinuated: the need for attention, or worrying about everything like some hysterical female. But there was a part of me that felt resigned. Going through all these appointments and tests—it was exhausting. I looked down at the referral and made a promise, not to her, but to myself, to call the therapist.

That was the last time I scheduled an appointment with Dr. Pitney. But it was the first time that her prescription would yield a positive change within me.

When I performed in *The Crucible* my sophomore year of high school, I experienced my first brush with the field of mental health. A friend of my mother's was dating a psychiatrist, and they all attended the play together. Afterward, over coffee and desserts, the boyfriend told my mother how hard it must be, raising a bipolar daughter.

"Pardon?"

"Your daughter. Clearly, she's bipolar."

"She was acting. Her character—Abigail Williams."

When my mother told me that story the next morning, she was fuming.

I thought it was the ultimate compliment. "Yeah! Even a psychiatrist thought my performance was authentic. I'm rockin' verisimilitude!"

Mom, however, remained loyally offended.

A few weeks afterward, the run of *The Crucible* ended at Grandstreet. No more pick-up rehearsals, no more clutching the script like a bible, no more late night woods scenes and courthouse trials with my band of followers. Camaraderie between cast members is one of the most powerful aspects of being in a play. We go through so much together: sweat, nervousness, tears, dropped lines, awkward blocking, sharp blocking, perfect timing, victory. When a play ends, the home that's been created shuts down too. The set is struck, the prop table disassembled, the dressing rooms cleared of costumes and makeup.

My dad noticed I was looking "down" after closing night, so he scheduled an appointment with a therapist in Helena—without telling me.

"But you've been acting so sad," he said in defense.

"Because I miss *The Crucible*, just like everyone else in my cast. Seriously, Dad."

I never went to the appointment, and my dad never brought it up again. Eventually, as I set my sights on the next play to audition for, the sadness dissolved as it always did. This instance, however, had been enough to set me against the idea of needing to "seek mental help."

Despite the stigma created in my youth, I scheduled a visit with the therapist Dr. Pitney recommended, a woman named Irene. Her office emitted a warm orange light. We sat, she in a plush chair and me on a couch. Irene had almond-shaped eyes wreathed in lashes. As I listened to her story, my trust in her grew. In an elegant accent, she described how she came to the United States from Argentina. She told me that she didn't emphasize diagnoses because "the name impedes progress." The patient could remain fixated on the label, creating what she called "a roadblock to recovery." She also believed in self-discovery, in having her patients connect the dots for themselves.

I told Irene a lot about my GI symptoms, and a little about the ship. "Everything—all my stomach problems started after I got back from... from...Oceans Abroad." I hadn't talked about the ship all summer, and just hearing those two words out loud made my throat tighten. I told her about falling ill on the ship and being misdiagnosed with heat rash, and about the dizziness and uncontrollable vomiting I experienced on Lariam.

"My dad lives by a lake," I said to Irene. "I was out there the other week, and...something happened." The house had an A-frame window and deck that faced the water. I'd been sitting on a couch in the living room, my feet propped on the coffee table. My dad was in the kitchen, talking on the phone to a golf buddy while he cooked dinner. I could hear the lemon potatoes sizzling in the oven. He measured nothing, just went by touch, smell. Bask the potatoes in olive oil, lemon, garlic powder, and crushed oregano. He was laughing, telling what sounded like a joke, until I heard him say, "They had to tether her to the ship's railing!"

I stared out the A-frame window, trying to block out his conversation. A speed boat zoomed by on the lake, hidden every few feet by the deck posts. I grabbed my water. The glass was cold. Too cold. I wanted to set it down, but I couldn't move my arm. Or my eyes. They were locked on the deck, trapped between the rails.

All I could hear were the waves.

All I could see was the ocean.

"I was there," I told Irene. "On deck. The crew was yelling at me to puke on the starboard side so I wouldn't be puking into the wind. But I wasn't puking...I was inside the house, on the couch, looking at the—the...."

Irene sat back in her chair. "When you experience trauma," she said, "certain triggers, like sounds or objects, can reactivate scenes from the event." She continued talking, but I stopped on that word, *trauma*. Wasn't trauma associated with severe physical accidents like car wrecks or head injuries?

Trauma comes from the Greek τραύμα, meaning "wound." It can occur from a single event, or from recurrent experiences that don't make sense, that don't fit into the spectrum of normal. The individual goes over the event again and again, scrutinizing every detail, trying to find some clue as to how it happened at all.

Irene went on to explain that psychological trauma can occur from events that threaten our physical or mental integrity. Experiences that blindside us, where we find ourselves powerless.

Isolated.

Neglected.

In a dark room.

Below deck.

For nine days.

Since returning from the ship, I had been suffering, unknowingly, from posttraumatic stress disorder. PTSD can occur in the military population or the general population, in males or females, in adults or even children. According to the *DSM-4*, the diagnostic manual in use in 2005, posttraumatic stress disorder could occur after witnessing or experiencing one or more events involving serious injury, threat of death, or threat to one's body. The disorder was characterized by reexperiencing the traumatic event, avoiding stimuli related to the trauma, and increased arousal. Not everyone who experiences trauma develops PTSD. I was one of the lucky ones.

I was lucky.

Despite what seemed like forever, I was diagnosed nineteen months after surviving a life-threatening event. Some people endure decades before their symptoms are traced back to trauma.

I was fortunate.

I had access to a therapist trained in trauma work. This type of therapy is a forte. Over the years, I've lived in numerous states and cities, so I've tried finding therapists to meet with in person. But I've always gone back to Irene, even if we can only have sessions over the phone, because she is an expert in trauma therapy.

When I read through my medical records in the fall of 2012, my last appointment with Dr. Pitney did, in fact, mention something related to PTSD. A portion of her report reads:

She still feels like she is having some anxiety and some posttraumatic stress changes after having had so many problems a year and a half ago when she was on a cruise. She feels like she does want to go into some counseling.

That old frustration surged through my temples. Several details struck me as careless, incongruous, and flat-out inaccurate:

First, Dr. Pitney never spoke the words "anxiety" or "posttraumatic stress" to me. What use did these crucial indicators have trapped in a medical file?

Second, I have never gone on a cruise in my life, nor do I have the desire to ever go on one. Oceans Abroad was not on a cruise ship with poolside drinks and nightly entertainers. It was on a working tall ship with masts and rigging.

Mincing words with a typed report dated 08/16/05 does little now. But it does make me wonder. What if Dr. Pitney had directly communicated her concern about PTSD to me? What if she had referred me to Irene immediately upon my return from Oceans Abroad? Would shame have infected my last semester of high school? Would I have stopped physically and emotionally punishing myself sooner? I see now more than ever the critical role primary care providers play in detecting mental illness.

I may never forgive Dr. Pitney for making me feel like I was being dismissed, or for calling me a hypochondriac. But my hope is that I serve as an example to other patients who grapple with ambiguous, undefined symptoms, and to the providers who treat them. The answer may be right there, where the patient has been pointing the entire time, or it may be in a whole other dimension altogether. One's being is a mosaic of pieces that, when looked at collectively, create a portrait. Examining one piece, while disregarding the whole, is like seeing a finger and not the sculptor, an ankle and not the dancer, a hernia and not the human being.

All I have to give are my tears. Will they be enough?
~Euripides, *Ifigeneia in Aulis*

M y therapy sessions with Irene went something like this: "I'm so mad! The way Brad and Jen are treated by the media. Does anyone ever think about how they feel? Their lives exploited!"

Brad Pitt and Jennifer Aniston, post-breakup, 2005.

In her plush chair, Irene listened to my tirade on American media and its invasiveness in celebrities' lives. When I finished, she asked, "Why do you think you are bothered by this?"

Squinting at the bookcase across from me, I tried to process her question. "The reason I am so upset is because...I feel like them. I feel like I'm in the spotlight—constantly. My family used to own Coney Island downtown, that hotdog and gyro place?" Irene nodded. "We grew up in the public's eye. 'You're a Perros.' 'How's your mom?' 'I remember when you were this high, bussing tables.' And everybody knows me from Grandstreet. 'When are you gonna be in another play?' I can't go anywhere without—I was hugged yesterday at the grocery store while buying tampons. What the hell? And I just took a job at a coffee shop—downtown—where I run into people I know every day. What was I thinking? I hate having to spend fall semester here with people asking me why I'm not at college."

Irene asked if what I felt was shame.

My shoulders dropped. My eyes welled. "Yes," I whispered. Tears slid down my cheeks and seeped into the corners of my mouth. Their saltiness reminded me of a dream I once had. A dream I'd been foolish enough to follow. "Why couldn't I have just stayed here?"

"Because," Irene said, "you have an adventurous spirit."

"That messed up my life."

A model ship rested on the bookshelf. Of all the decorations to put in a therapist's office, why was one of them a goddamn ship? I had an urge to hurl my purse at it.

"People," Irene said, "are too busy with their own lives to remember what happened in someone else's."

I tore my eyes away from the ship. "You think so?"

"Of course."

Above the ship, a clock ticked. Our hour was almost up, yet I felt no closer to forgiving my adventurous spirit.

In 2013, the American Psychiatric Association published its fifth edition of the *Diagnostic and Statistical Manual of Mental Disorders*. In the *DSM-5*, a new symptom cluster was added to PTSD: "negative alterations in cognitions and mood." Symptoms include persistent "exaggerated negative beliefs or expectations about oneself," "distorted cognitions about the cause or consequences of the traumatic event(s) that lead the individual to blame himself/herself," and a "negative emotional state (e.g., fear, horror, anger, guilt, or shame)."

Negative beliefs or expectations about yourself.

Self-blame.

Anger.

Self-inflicted shame.

I was almost twenty-eight years old when this edition was released, nine years after the ship. As I read and reread those words, I felt something I'd never felt before. The self-defeating thoughts of weakness, the belief that my body had failed me, the feeling that I had let down my entire Greek lineage, the punishment of pounding out miles on a treadmill, the shame that kept me from confiding in my peers—these are common responses for people who've experienced trauma, so much so that the American Psychiatric Association added them to its revised criteria. Other people who've endured trauma cope in the same way. Despite having a mental health disorder, I didn't feel so alone. I felt, somehow, recognized.

DATE OF STUDY: 08/24/05
[DOPPLER] ABDOMEN ULTRASOUND:
HISTORY: Check portal vein patency.
FINDINGS: The portal vein is patent, hepatic veins are patent. The liver is of normal size. There is hepatofugal flow. The gallbladder has normal wall thickness with fasting distention and contains a 2 mm posterior polyp, but no stones.
IMPRESSION:
I.   GALLBLADDER POLYP, OTHERWISE NEGATIVE.

Located on the right side of a person's torso, the gallbladder is a small organ connected to the liver and pancreas. It stores extra bile that is eventually released into the small intestine. An evolutionary conundrum, the gallbladder is not a necessary organ in humans. It aids in digestion, especially of fatty foods, but can be removed with little ill effect on the digestive tract.

A gallbladder polyp is a tab that forms on the wall of the gallbladder. Conclusive research about gallbladder polyps was scarce, so Dr. Ake Andren-Sandberg of Stockholm, Sweden, synthesized eleven years' worth of medical studies. Andren-Sandberg states that the objective of his research is to help physicians with how to "handle the next patient with gallbladder polyp." Polyps don't usually cause symptoms, but he explains that "if any symptoms are caused, most commonly right upper quadrant pain, nausea, dyspepsia [indigestion], and jaundice are seen."

Usually gallstones are the cause of gallbladder attacks. Since no gallstones were found in my Doppler ultrasound, something else was

causing my abdominal attacks. The polyp may have been contribut-
ing to the backup of fluid the MR cholangiography detected, which
can cause gallbladder attacks similar to those instigated by gallstones.
Because the gallbladder is not necessary to live, when people have
symptomatic polyps or gallstones, common practice is to surgically
remove the gallbladder altogether, thus eliminating any chance of
repeat symptoms or future complications. The thought of surgery did
not scare me; the unpredictability of my abdominal attacks did. No
matter what anyone says to you, the effects of chronic GI problems
are lifestyle-debilitating, and I was tired of being treated like they
weren't. I wanted my life back. I wanted to be healthy and active, and
if an unneeded organ was impeding my path to physical freedom,
then it ought to be removed.

Date of Service: 09/07/05
Attending Physician: Dr. Spencer, Gastroenterologist
*Jamie returns today for follow-up of her abdominal pain. She contin-
ues to complain of some right upper quadrant abdominal pain. She saw
a naturopath, and has had some dietary changes, which have decreased
her bloating. In addition, she has evolved into more of a chronic diarrhea
picture. In the past, where she would have constipation alternating with
diarrhea, she now has fairly persistent diarrhea. She will have up to 3 bowel
movements a day and these are typically watery. There has been no blood.
Her weight has been stable, and actually has increased somewhat. Her
appetite continues to be poor.*

*She is scheduled to go to art school in January, and does not plan on
returning to Helena for a prolonged period. Currently, she is eating rice and
vegetables most of the time, since this seems to control her symptoms.*

*Laboratory studies and data have been reviewed with the patient. Most
recently, we did an MR cholangiogram, which showed a possible filling
defect in the liver and some free fluid overlying the right lobe of the liver.
This was followed up with a dedicated ultrasound with Doppler but there
is no evidence of any thrombosis [blood clot]. There was a gallbladder polyp
noted.*

IMPRESSION

1. *Gallbladder polyp. We have discussed the implications of this.*

2. *Abdominal pain. I really continue to think that this represents IBS; however, I suppose it is possible there is a component of her pain caused by gallbladder disease.*

3. *Diarrhea. This seems to be developing into more of a chronic picture and seems to be more severe than previously.*

PLAN

1. *Given the patient's change in symptoms, I have recommended a colonoscopy to rule out any colonic pathology. Random biopsies will be obtained to evaluate for microscopic colitis.*

2. *Continue current dietary interventions.*

3. *The patient would like to see a surgeon if her colonoscopy is unremarkable, and I think this is probably reasonable. I will set her up for a surgical referral pending the results of the colonoscopy.*

I never went in for the colonoscopy. I never made it past what Harvard Medical School's *Family Health Guide* calls "the purgative part: taking a powerful bowel-clearing substance and coping with the resulting diarrhea." I've "coped" with plenty of diarrhea in my life. What I couldn't cope with were the laxatives. Because my intestines were so out of sync, the first dose made my insides feel like they were being scraped out with a scythe. The second dose I poured down the sink. The morning of the procedure, I listened to my gut and took charge of my health: I canceled the colonoscopy. I got a referral to a surgeon. A month later, I had gallbladder surgery and haven't had an acute abdominal attack since.

Could Lariam have led to my gallbladder disease? Mefloquine is processed in the liver and excreted in the bile, and the liver supplies bile to the gallbladder, but this is as far as I can trace any cause or effect between the drug and my biliary symptoms.

Laparoscopic comes from the ancient Greek λαπάρα (lapara), or "soft part of the body," and σκοπέω (skopio), the verb "to see." In a laparoscopic gallbladder surgery, surgical instruments are inserted through your abdomen, and a camera projects your innards onto a video screen for the surgeon.

At the end of October 2005, at an outpatient clinic in Helena, I went under general anesthesia and was placed onto an operating table. A scalpel was used to cut a crescent-shaped incision near my bellybutton. A tube called a trocar was inserted through the slit. Carbon dioxide was pumped through the trocar, inflating my belly to maximize visibility of the organs. A video camera traveled down the tube. The surgical team inserted two more trocars below the right side of my ribcage and one trocar below my sternum. Forceps and other instruments entered through these ports. The instruments were used to separate the tissue that adheres the gallbladder to the liver. Before removing the gallbladder, the surgeon clamped both the cystic duct and the cystic artery with small permanent titanium clamps. My gallbladder was then detached, placed into a specimen bag, and removed through one of the ports. The trocars were taken out, the carbon dioxide expelled from my belly, and the four incisions sutured.

Like the typical textbook case, I was home by afternoon and back to work within two weeks. But I was not typical. I was headstrong and ambitious. I needed to be in California—performance ready—in two months. My diaphragm needed to be prepared for musical theatre, my muscles fit for stage combat, and my abdominal core conditioned for dance. I was so close to finally pursuing my passions, except I had four abdominal incisions and layer upon layer of scar tissue to heal.

I worked at Fire Tower Coffeehouse. The shop was on Helena's main street, named Last Chance Gulch, which harkens back to the gold rush days. In the summer of 1864, four miners were about to give up on the creek bed of what is now the downtown. Deciding to give the waters one last chance, they struck gold. The coffeehouse was named after a fire tower coined the Guardian of the Gulch. Built about a decade after the miners struck gold, the fire tower observed Helena transform from a raucous boomtown into a refined state capital. The twenty-five-foot tower is still visible from the downtown and was a favorite retreat of mine in high school. My friends and I used to drive up Cruse Avenue and park in the small lot. Even in the winter, we'd sit on the snow beneath the tower and watch the Montana sky turn star-studded. Every Thanksgiving weekend, a holiday arts festival stretching the length of Last Chance Gulch was held in honor of the fire tower. Hot cocoa in hand, we'd count down to the lighting of our vigilante version of a Christmas tree.

A few weeks after surgery, I was working the breakfast shift. It must've been a Saturday or Sunday because the coffeehouse was slammed. Condensation fogged the windows. The bells on the door jingled every time a new pack of customers entered. Each of us was assigned a task: Linda at the cash register, Haley in the kitchen, and me operating the espresso machine. But sometimes our roles got jumbled. If Linda was restocking the juice cooler, I took orders. If I needed to run a bagel back to Haley, Linda pumped chocolate syrup into the cups. If Haley had a line of food orders ready, Linda and I delivered plates to tables.

The drink orders were mounting: hot chocolate with soymilk, nonfat latte, sugar-free vanilla chai, peppermint mocha, mocha breve, peach smoothie, caramel steamer, extra foam cappuccino. I ground espresso beans, pulled shots, steamed milk, measured smoothie syrup, poured the shots into paper cups, stirred the caramel, mixed the powdered cocoa, measured half a cup of ice, turned on the blender, poured the steamed milk, spooned the foam. I was managing fine, until I wasn't. As much as I have played, paused, and rewound this day in my head, I cannot isolate the tipping point. There was no trigger—nothing that flung me back to the ship. I remained in the present, but was unable to function in it. Instead of a gold pan with a mesh sifter separating dust from pebbles, pebbles from rocks—background murmur from chatter, chatter from noise—there was none. The rocks dropped right into my ears: grinding beans, whirring milk, blending ice, scraping chairs, screaming kids, clanking spoons, clanking glasses, ringing cash register, ringing phones, ringing bells.

My body turned to stone. Hands rigid, back stiff.

"Jamie, can you get that shot?"

That shot?

That shot?

Linda's voice sounded like it was echoing down a mine shaft.

Finally, my posture broke.

"I can't *do* this."

I fled, darting between chairs and coats, bumping into people I knew and drinks I'd just poured. I slammed the bathroom door behind me and sank to the floor. I elbowed the garbage can, which toppled over with a soft thud. I hit the toilet paper, which unwound into a pool of white. I tried inhaling slowly, but my breaths quickened. Tears mingled with drool as I gasped for air. My hands pressed my wet temples together, trying to keep my head from exploding. I needed Irene. I needed help. I needed to find a way to protect myself from the chaos blasting through my brain.

A light knocking sounded on the door.

My eyes bolted to the metal handle.

"May I come in?" Haley called.

Haley had long dreadlocks and a solid presence. She was confident, a natural leader. Reaching up, I turned the handle. She walked in and sat on the floor across from me, as if leaning against the wall in a single bathroom cubicle was as common as sitting on a couch.

"I'm sorry," I said before she could say anything. "I'm just—" I searched for an all-encompassing word—"overwhelmed."

"It's okay," she said. "It's slammed out there."

"It's not just that."

"I know. You just had surgery. Don't beat yourself up."

How'd she know I'm hard on myself?

"You gotta respect your body, take care of it."

"But I can't do anything I used to!" I threw a roll of toilet paper. We watched it bounce off the wall and roll under the sink.

"I know what you're going through," she said. "I played basketball in high school and couldn't stand it when my ankle went out. Injury after injury. It drove me nuts. But you gotta relax. You can't push it. It's only gonna make things worse. Your body—it's your temple."

I was about to insult the cliché, but something stopped me. I didn't hear just Haley's words; I heard, within them, a tone of reverence. A reverence I had been desecrating since returning from the ship. My body was not a failed instrument. My body was a sacred space that housed my spirit, and I had been blaming it for something out of its control for far too long.

It began then, in that bathroom painted midnight blue. A new perspective started to give light, a discarding of old beliefs and habits that no longer helped me. I wish I could say this small breakthrough completely reversed my thoughts and actions. But that's not how inner change works. Nor is that how healing from trauma works. The pace is slow but sure, a thin thread of light that, through much practice, slowly begins to shine.

When I relayed the Fire Tower episode to Irene, she asked which hand, my left or my right, had been doing most of the work. "At the espresso station, I remember reaching across my body with my right hand to get a spoon, even though the spoons were on my left." I also told her how I hesitated to grab a food order with my left hand, even when my right hand was already holding a plate.

Irene propped a legal pad on her knees and drew a large X. "The left side of the brain controls the *right* hand," she explained. "And the right side of the brain controls the *left* hand." On a new sheet of paper, she drew a blob with a line through it. "The right brain," she said, pointing with her pen, "controls emotions, creativity, and abstract concepts." She pointed to the other side. "The left brain is logical and needs facts. With PTSD, there is a split between the two hemispheres. They are not united. Since the ship, you have stopped trusting your right brain...your emotions, your intuition, your creativity." She flipped back to the X. "So you have stopped using your left hand."

As Irene pointed out, the brain's hemispheres differ significantly. The left brain controls one's verbal logic, linear categorization, and scientific and mathematical skills. It is literal and relies on facts, organization, and tangible events. The right brain is figurative, intuitive, and imaginative. It's where creativity is manifested, as well as emotional expression and the ability to empathize. When a person is healthy, the brain's hemispheres operate as a unified whole. When a person undergoes trauma, discord ensues.

Trauma jilts the brain, causing what is called a functional split. This split occurs so the individual can continue functioning in day-to-day life. Memories from the traumatic event or events are separated into different parts of the brain in order to protect the individual from remembering what happened. Despite these efforts to protect its cognitive integrity, the brain remains in conflict. The right hemisphere can feel intense emotions, but is unable to connect them to an event. It reacts to certain stimuli but cannot understand why something incites a certain reaction, be it crying at the sight of a mother or cowering in the face of flashing lights. Similarly, the left hemisphere needs proof of the event, but cannot access any. This lack of evidence frustrates the left side as it tries to make sense of the fear but is unable to do so.

How, then, do you reestablish harmony? How do you re-bridge the right and left hemispheres of the brain? In our therapy session, Irene guided me through exercises that focused on my left hand to reactivate the emotional, intuitive right brain. She had me hold a glass of water with my left hand and bring it to my lips.

You're going to spill. Don't spill. Give me the glass. You're going to spill!

"What's going on now?" Irene asked.

I set the glass onto the table. "I keep thinking I'll spill all over."

"That is your left brain criticizing your right," Irene explained. "Your left brain took over after the ship. You went on autopilot. Now, it is time to break its control and start trusting your emotional side once more."

Next, Irene instructed me to hold two small weighted spheres in my left hand and roll them around in my palm. "How do you feel?" she asked.

"Like I'm going to drop them."

Then she had me rotate the spheres in my right hand.

"Oh, this is way easier."

"We need to rebuild your left hand's confidence," Irene said. She told me to give my left hand responsibilities at work: scoop the ice with my left arm, hold cups in my left hand, turn on the blender with my left index finger. To activate both hemispheres of the brain, she recommended exercises that require both hands like playing the piano or passing a ball from palm to palm. She also recommended I take walks outside without any set path: "Do not decide beforehand where to go. When you come to a fork in the road, go where your intuition tells you to, wherever you feel drawn." This exercise would soon become my favorite way of reconnecting with my intuitive self.

Irene's lesson about the brain's hemispheres helped me understand my struggles in *Barnum* the summer before. My inability to connect to my character was influenced by a symptom of PTSD called emotional numbing. Because my right brain was dormant, I was unable to access positive emotions like happiness, joy, or optimism. How could I have felt these emotions as my character if I couldn't even feel them for myself?

I also began to understand why I never mastered juggling. While the rest of the cast learned how to juggle, I never improved at it, even when I used scarves instead of beanbags. Juggling requires both hands—and both hemispheres of the brain—to work together. Instead of alternating the scarves between my hands, my right hand had tried to do everything. I remember grabbing a scarf on my right side and reaching across my chest to catch a scarf on my left. The more frustrated I became from not being able to juggle, the more the critical left brain dominated my *thought patterns* until all I could hear were self-sabotaging thoughts of physical inadequacy.

Irene also helped me connect the dots between the disorder and my gastrointestinal reactions. Symptoms such as stomachache or diarrhea may actually be what are called secondary illnesses, seemingly unrelated conditions caused by the primary illness. Secondary illnesses of PTSD include a range of symptoms, from GI problems and chronic muscular aches, to increased heart rate and high blood pressure.

Secondary illnesses are often left misdiagnosed or undiagnosed. Doctors may mislabel these symptoms if their sight is too myopic. They may fail to consider the relationship between organ systems and life experiences. Shame, privacy, or an inability to recall a traumatic event contributes to patients' own shortsightedness. They may not be aware that a traumatic event is somehow related to their symptoms, or that they even experienced trauma, as was the case with me.

Irene saw my physical symptoms from a different perspective. She was the first health care professional who traced my symptoms back to my past.

My GI problems still haven't been resolved. I still have chronic diarrhea and constipation, still cramp up with lower abdominal pain. I've been diagnosed with irritable bowel syndrome by GI specialists across the nation. But that's not all I have. That's not the whole story. Cramps, diarrhea—they're often triggered by stimuli that sound, look, or feel like being back on the *SV Interlude*.

In the summer of 2012, Luke was on his psychiatry rotation in medical school, shadowing a psychiatrist named Dr. Bachman. I was in research mode that summer, trying to better understand the relationship between PTSD and the gastrointestinal system. With a list of questions I gave him, Luke sat down with Dr. Bachman on my behalf. Luke had asked me if I wanted to talk to her instead, but I wasn't ready to.

Dr. Bachman explained to Luke that when a person is under attack, the left brain's fight-or-flight response enacts the sympathetic nervous system. The sympathetic nervous system increases heart rate, blood pressure, and gland excretion. It also slows down the digestive tract. As a result, a person becomes constipated.

Once a person is no longer under immediate threat, the parasympathetic nervous system takes over, which decreases the heart rate, eases the smooth muscles lining the intestines, and relaxes the sphincter. The digestive tract finally unconstricts, causing diarrhea.

Someone who has endured trauma fluctuates between relaxation and tension. Memories and sensory stimuli can reactivate that sense of immediate threat, switching the body back into fight-or-flight mode and upsetting the balance of the bowels once more. This may be a reason why people with PTSD also have IBS.

What I believe, more than any research I've found, is that any experience that rattles the ground beneath your feet also rattles your mind and body. When the body and mind are jilted, you don't need scientific proof to know that what you're feeling is real.

It was a crisp November morning, not long after my Fire Tower episode. I'm not sure why, but I was telling Irene about my fascination with dolphins.

When I was little, I was in love with dolphins. I had dolphin necklace charms, dolphin key chains, dolphin calendars. I checked out every book on dolphins, pouring over diagrams of their bones. Did you know that dolphins have five fingers in their fins, they have ball-and-socket joints, and their spinal column is flexible, just like ours? They are intelligent, crave social interaction, and become depressed when separated from their pod. Forget monkeys—I descended from dolphins!

My fascination with dolphins continued into adulthood. In college, I took an astronomy class and completed a research project on Delphinus, a constellation in the sky's northern hemisphere. In one myth about the constellation's origin, a celebrated poet named Arion traveled from Korinth to Sicily to spread his fame. On his return sail, he caught wind that his crew was plotting to toss him overboard and divvy up his spoils. As a last request, Arion asked if he might don his singing robes and perform a final song before casting himself into the sea. The crew consented. Thus, the most moving dirge was played upon Arion's lyre. As the last note strained the air, Arion threw himself into the water. His song, however, enchanted a pod of dolphins who had appeared along the prow of the ship. One of the dolphins bore him to safe shores. In honor of both, Apollo placed the dolphin in the sea of stars, where Delphinus could eternally watch over poets.

During our therapy session, Irene said that dolphins might be my totem animal. Except something didn't make sense.

"Tell me, what's going on right now?" Irene asked.

"If I'm so much like a dolphin, then why was I unable to survive at sea?" I realized I was standing, my fists clenched.

"You weren't at the sea."

My nostrils flared. "Fine. The ocean. Whatever."

"No. You were not at the sea." She propped a legal pad on her slacks and drew a squiggly line. "You were *on* it. Where do dolphins live?"

I sat down, reluctant but drawn into her visual lesson. "In the sea."

"Yes," she said, pointing below the squiggly line. "*In* the sea. If you take the strongest dolphin in the ocean and put her on the deck of a boat, what happens?"

I imagined a dolphin thumping against hard planks, water dripping from her gleaming skin, her magnificently arched body helpless, defenseless against her environment. "She can't survive."

"When taken out of their natural habitat," Irene said, "even the strongest animals in the world cannot survive. Does that make the dolphin any less strong?"

"No," I whispered.

"Does that make you any less strong?"

My breath caught in my throat.

"Jamie, you were not weak for being unable to survive on that ship."

I nodded, believing for the first time that weakness had nothing to do with who I was.

When I turned eight, my dad gave me a ring shaped like a dolphin. I used to try it on each of my fingers, but it always slipped to the side. After my session with Irene, I searched under my bed and found the ring. It fit perfectly. I've worn it ever since, a totem reminding me of the innate power of my favorite animal.

GAMMA

Climax:
the brink of
crashing or soaring

ΓΙΙ

After being on guard all night, I must learn how to rest.

~Aristofanes, *Wasps*

I promised myself I wouldn't romanticize college in California. I wouldn't revere the cavernous dance studios, dedicated professors, or velvet-curtained stage. I wouldn't admire the palm trees lining the footpaths, the rose garden once tended by Franciscan priests, or the vines clinging to the white stucco walls and red tiled roofs. But I couldn't help it. Dreaming was part of my very being. Without dreaming and believing, I wouldn't have gotten this far.

Winter quarter began in early January, when a cool haze clung to the air. The university was located about an hour from San Francisco. I shared a house with two women three blocks from campus. An alumna of the university owned the house and had converted it into an eco-friendly vegan home. She lived in a yellow bedroom off the kitchen, another housemate lived in the red bedroom, and I lived in the bedroom painted Grannie Smith green. "The Orchard," she proudly called her home. The back porch overlooked a garden. The front porch opened to a congested city street. Though I spent most of my time at home or on campus, the commotion of urban life would eventually flood my three-block radius of familiarity.

I had taken half a year off from college, but I wanted to catch up and finish in four years, so I enrolled in as many courses as I could: literature, poetry, religious studies, theatre history, and acting. At the last minute, I switched the acting course to a modern dance class. I wasn't sure why I did this. It just felt safer.

My mother had minored in modern dance in college. I liked the idea of following in her footsteps, of sculpting my body into similar forms. I'd thought about taking ballet, but the rigidity and constriction made me think twice. Ballet required pink tights, and I had been unable to wear tight clothing around my waist since having gallbladder surgery. The incision near my belly button felt like a rod puncturing deep into my core, and a taut waistband would only push that rod deeper. Required attire for modern was bare feet and loose clothing. No cramming into canvas ballet slippers; no cinching them tighter to simulate a perfect point. We could wear whatever we wanted, as long as our clothing didn't limit our movement. I opted for a seamless leotard to avoid a bra band from touching the incision below my sternum, and loose cotton capri pants. Feeling the wooden floor beneath my feet was a new sensation. I'd always worn black character shoes—high heels with a buckled strap around the ankle—in plays and musicals. Without any shoes on, my toes spread onto the ground.

The dance studio was high-ceilinged, with large mirrors spanning the entire length of the walls. Just above the mirrors, rectangular windows stretched across, spilling bands of natural light onto the wood floor. A grand piano stood in a corner, complete with a live pianist. I noticed that he improvised to our movements reflecting in the mirrors. I'd studied piano from elementary through high school, but I could never just sit down at the bench and start playing without sheet music. My piano teacher had taught me classical technique and theory, so I took my cues from Beethoven and Bach. The pianist took his cues from our professor, Olivia Valentine.

Olivia had the shiniest black hair I'd ever seen. As she led our class through warm-ups, it slipped over her shoulders like feathers on a raven. I'd never had a dance instructor who didn't pull her hair into a tight bun. Modern dance, it seemed, demanded no such strictness. Olivia usually wore a rust-colored sweater she tossed aside halfway through warm-ups. She moved like a child: innocent, sure-footed, trusting.

"She has the complexion of Snow White," a new friend of mine whispered. We were stretching with the rest of the class. I nodded upside down, brushing my fingertips to the floor as we hung in a hamstring stretch.

"Have you seen her baby?"

I rolled up one vertebra at a time. "She has a baby?"

"Yeah, she was on maternity leave last year."

I peeked through the lines of dancers to get a better look at our professor. Her figure betrayed no roundness of the belly, no strain in the back from having carried a child for nine months. If she could give birth and be back in the studio, surely I could have surgery and perform two months later. But Olivia was a professional dancer; I was an impatient postadolescent with an invincibility complex.

One afternoon, Olivia instructed all fifty of us to sit on the floor. "Now, take your right foot in your hands and begin massaging."

I looked around. My peers were hunched over their legs, grabbing their feet and kneading. Frowning, I pulled my ankle toward me and noticed the dirt my heel had picked up from the studio floor. *This is absurd*, I thought. *Backs and leg muscles need massaging, not feet.*

"Begin at the ankle," Olivia instructed. "Gently rotate it around, and feel it loosen. Now, work that tendon between your fingers. Feel how tender it is on either side. Slow circles up to your calf, now down to the base of your heel. Stay there a moment." I had never massaged my feet, let alone the base of my heel. I was surprised at how much feeling it had.

"We need to appreciate our feet," Olivia called, her voice echoing up to the ceiling. "They carry us to our dreams. They lead us home. They endure so much and ask so little in return." As I massaged each squatty toe, I thought about Olivia's words. When had I ever thanked my feet for getting me off the ship? When had I thanked them for carrying me through the hallways when I returned to high school amid rumors and shame? When had I ever thanked my feet for their steadfast devotion to my passions? My feet had brought me here, despite a drug reaction, mental disorder, and laparoscopic surgery, to a performing arts program in California.

Before starting college, my mother had given me a book filled with quotes about dance. After class that evening, I found one from Martha Graham, mother of modern dance: *Think of the magic of that foot, comparatively small, upon which your whole weight rests. It's a miracle, and the dance is a celebration of that miracle.* I didn't realize it then, but honoring my feet was one of the best things I could've done on my path toward healing. Dancing barefoot helped me feel more grounded, and for someone whose trauma occurred on top of water, rebuilding a connection to solid ground was vital.

One afternoon, I decided to visit Olivia in her office. I didn't expect her to know me. I wasn't a standout dancer in her class. The students who'd been classically trained in ballet stood out, whereas the theatre majors, like me, acted through each routine, compensating for not having proper technique.

"Jamie, so nice to see you. Please, sit." She motioned to a soft chair.

As I rambled on about how freeing modern dance was, I realized I was stalling. The real reason I'd stopped by her office was to take some responsibility for my body. "I just had surgery," I told her, "which is why I'm not moving as well as I used to."

"You are naturally graceful," Olivia said, "but I can see you are a little guarded."

I noticed I was hugging my torso, trying to encompass all four incisions in a wrapped embrace. I don't remember if I told her anything more about my injury, but I remember something she said that didn't make sense at the time.

"You will become a wiser performer," Olivia told me. "You will become more selective with what you devote your energy to."

I didn't want to be selective. I wanted to explore modern and jazz and musical theatre. I wanted to act and sing. I wanted to audition for a dance troupe, and maybe even take a choreography class next quarter. But as Olivia said, I did not have an infinite supply of energy. When I wasn't on campus, I was usually propped up in bed, completing homework and restoring my muscles so I'd have enough energy for the next day's dance class.

By the end of January, I had joined two dance clubs and signed up to assistant stage-manage the spring dance concert. Watching the dancers from backstage became the highlight of my nights. The student dancers were so agile. Their pirouettes looked effortless, their postures erect, their shoulders and hips perfectly aligned. The more I became involved with dance, the more I felt my ties to theatre loosening. Theatre was the reason why I transferred here, what I received a scholarship in, what I had been doing since childhood. But it wasn't nurturing my body the way that dance was beginning to.

For modern, we were required to attend a concert. At the end of January, a handful of friends and I drove to Palo Alto for a Martha Graham Dance Company show. The concert included a piece called "Cave of the Heart," which depicted the ancient Greek tragedy of Medea. Overcome by love, Medea helps Jason steal the golden fleece and seeks exile with him in Korinth. Soon after, he abandons her for the princess of Korinth, which is where the Graham piece began. The dancer who played Medea moved with such power. Tension was visible in every tendon of her body, from her neck to her forearms to her forced arch. Each step pounded the floor, and each turn pierced with precision. In spite of her strength, Medea fell victim to her own passion and in the end, destroyed herself and those around her. What I took from the piece was that passion exists solely to devour and tear apart.

The piece's message paralleled what I'd been learning in my theatre history class. The course was an overview of performance art from the end of the Middle Ages to the Romantic Period. In the seventeenth century, theatre experienced a rebirth of classical ideals. French playwright Jean Racine wrote *Phèdre*, based on Euripides's ancient tragedy *Hippolytos*. More so than the original, Racine's version exposed the destabilizing nature of passion. Through a dizzying plot of lust, lies, and violence, the overall message of the play was that unruly passions must be controlled; otherwise, they would cause personal or social destruction, just as Medea's passion had.

I felt the destabilizing nature of passion every time I approached the stage. Each night before dance concert rehearsals, I arrived early to sweep the auditorium floor. Whenever I stepped onstage, a mixture of desire and fear seized me. I wanted so badly to perform, to be under the lights, but my body was not ready. I was not ready. As Olivia had reminded me, I was still recovering from surgery. I was still recovering from trauma. It had been exactly two years since the ship, and I was finally beginning to emotionally reconnect with myself and my surroundings, but the process was confusing. I felt unnerved. The stage had been my home for nearly half my life, yet it was producing such an uncharacteristic sense of fear within me. The thought of being in front of a packed auditorium didn't excite me anymore; it terrified me. All those faces judging me, watching my every move, hearing my every word. I felt estranged from the stage, homesick, longing for a place I could not reenter.

When the dance concert opened to the public, I was relieved to be a stage manager and not a performer. I rarely left my tech booth behind the dark curtains. Yet even from backstage, the lights shone too brightly. The applause echoed too loudly. When I closed my eyes, the clapping sounded like crashing waves. The soft murmuring of the dancers offstage reminded me that I was in the auditorium at college, not trapped on the sea.

Since I could not cross the threshold, I wrote. In my poetry class, I composed a poem called "Incessant," about the emotional abuse of self-criticism; a poem called "Walk as Though with Child," about the tenderness needed to heal after surgery; and a poem titled "Places":

house lights fade to black
overture begins
curtains roll to proscenium
chorus rushes on

stage lights up
And
she remains offstage

watching the procession
swaying with the beat
hearing for her vamp

once
twice
One More Time

she remains offstage

it's not that she doesn't know her part
she knows it to the core
she Hears it
Tastes it
Drinks it
Sleeps it
Breathes it

it's that she can't
face
the Brilliance

shining in stage lights
resounding in tumultuous applause

take but one step
and enter cosmic array
Or
remain backstage
spectator to creation

Every week, I had a phone session with Irene. We continued my PTSD therapy, me sitting in my bed and she in her office. Many of our sessions addressed my frustration over not being as active as I had been before the ship.

"You must follow your natural rhythm," Irene told me one afternoon. "How is the environment around you?"

I held the cell phone to my ear, thinking how unlike nature the city was. "It's loud. I have to walk by this busy street on my way to campus every day. I kind of—I don't know—freeze up." My legs stopped moving. My intestines squeezed. When I walked next to traffic, the cars zoomed at me head-on. The motion and noise ignited a fear that melded with the fears in my memory. The car engines sounded like the droning ship engine. The clanking metal on semitrucks sounded like the metal bunk room doors that slammed shut. The entire quarters below deck were made of metal—metal stairs leading down, metal panels running along the narrow corridor, metal coat hooks. Loud, hard metal.

"How are you eating?"

Irene's voice tore me out of the past. "Healthy—I'm eating healthy. My housemate works at a grocery store, so she brings home bruised fruit and dented cans and stuff."

Irene waited. Somehow she always knew when there was more.

"Well," I said, "I'm always hungry when I shouldn't be. Like late at night. If I go to bed hungry, I can't fall asleep. But I'm afraid that if I eat right before bed, I'll get acid reflux."

"You are not a robot," Irene said. She told me that our bodies do not obey a regimented breakfast-lunch-dinner schedule. "Eat when you are hungry, not when the clock says you are 'supposed' to."

"But eating at midnight isn't good for you."

"Think of nature," Irene countered. "Animals eat any time of the day, depending on their natural rhythm. Owls eat at night because they are nocturnal. Lions eat whenever they find food because they are hunters. When does the dolphin eat?"

"I don't know."

"When she is hungry."

I looked at the dolphin ring wrapped around my finger. Then I glanced at the closed door to my room and the windows covered with thick shades. "Sometimes," I told Irene, "I worry that I can't adapt. To anything. Like I can't live in cities or anywhere that might trigger my PTSD." I twisted the ring around my finger. "It makes me feel *weak*."

I whispered that last awful *w-* word.

"Give me the name of a strong plant."

"A—a cactus."

"Where does a cactus live?" Irene asked.

"In the desert."

"What would happen if the cactus were planted in the jungle?"

"It'd get all soggy and droopy."

"Is the cactus weak because it cannot survive in the jungle?"

"No, it's just not in the right environment."

"Exactly." Irene told me that I, like the cactus, needed to be aware of what environment suited me. She told me to use nature as a guide. While I walked to campus, she said to notice the green veins in the leaves, the orange petals of the flowers, and the woven bark of the tree trunks. I could even walk on the grassy boulevard instead of the concrete sidewalk to feel more connected to the earth. This exercise would help me recognize how many things are the opposite of metal, the opposite of floating on the sea, of not feeling solid ground beneath my feet.

In California, I did not have the knowledge of trauma research to help me understand, on an intellectual level, my physical responses to the environment around me. I knew my reaction to urban life had something to do with PTSD because I was not afraid of cities before the ship. Now I know that much of what I was experiencing had to do with a symptom of post-trauma called hyperarousal. A defense mechanism, hyperarousal causes a person to have an amplified awareness of sensory stimuli. As the *DSM-5* describes, individuals with PTSD often display "a heightened sensitivity to potential threats." In the brain, the amygdala instigates this hyper-alertness. Eyes notice the slightest movements. Ears hear the faintest sounds. People are especially aware of stimuli that remind them of past life-threatening experiences.

In the face of danger, humans are programmed by evolution to flee or fight. But what happens when they are trapped, unable to run, kick, or punch? With traumatic events, people are unable to prevent what is about to occur. When a person's natural responses to danger are blocked, there is no sense of release from the traumatic event, no conclusion, no closure. The person continues to probe the environment for external threats long after the event has passed.

Even years later, people can involuntarily reenter this state of enhanced readiness, as I did every time I stepped outside The Orchard. My sense of hearing was most amplified, probably because during those nine days in a dark bunk room, my ears had been the one sense able to gather information about my surroundings. Honking, zooming, clanking, slamming, droning, lurching, screeching—noise triggered a fear that spliced the past into the present.

After my classes, I usually stopped by the university's chapel before walking home. For over a hundred years this mission church had stood, beholding Mexico's independence from Spain, secularization, the Gold Rush, and the beginnings of a college. I've always felt an affinity for timeworn structures. Whenever I see Montana's state capitol or Grandstreet Theatre or a Greek Orthodox church, I am struck by the sheer mass of history. That same awe lured me to the mission church on campus. In my youth, I didn't spend a lot of time in churches, mainly when my family traveled back to the Midwest to visit relatives. Unlike Orthodox churches, the university's chapel had no central dome or Byzantine-styled icons encircling the interior. Instead, it had a high flat ceiling and pale walls. When I walked through the iron-hinged doors, my eyes had to adjust to the dim lighting. I always sat to the right, in a row of wooden chairs to myself. Sometimes tears slipped down my cheeks; other times I lifted my eyes to the ceiling, taking in its vastness. I felt secure inside the church, but unsafe the farther I traveled from my three-block radius of familiarity.

As candles flickered at the altar, I contemplated what it meant to heal. I contemplated the definition of success, which didn't seem conducive to healing. In my teens, I had equated success with grade point averages, which role I had in a play, how many extracurricular activities I could pack in after school. Success, back then, had nothing to do with maintaining inner harmony or outer health. I was beginning to understand that being at a reputable college meant little more than a line on a resume if that school wasn't the best fit for me. My mind was restless, my body in fear of its environment, my heart in search of friends I had in Oregon and family I had in Montana. The greatest success I could achieve was not securing superficial titles, materialistic status symbols, or whatever else I thought was valued by society; the greatest success I could achieve was to recover from trauma.

Staring at a painting of Mary, I prayed for gentleness. I kissed my fingertips to each scar on my torso. I pressed a hand to my heart, reminding myself that it was safe to feel. "*I am on my side,*" I whispered to Mary. "*I am on my side.*"

In early March, one of my dance clubs was scheduled to perform at the chapel for a night mass. The club taught liturgical dancing, an integration of movement and religious expression. There were about ten of us, led by a senior dance major. She choreographed a routine to the song "Wade in the Water." We practiced in pastel blue leotards with flowy pants. When we rehearsed in the dance studio, I paid little attention to the lyrics.

At mass, the words and crowded rows of people consumed me. The chapel was so packed we barely had enough space to complete our lunges and pirouettes. My costume, which had reminded me of soft sky, stung like ice on my thighs. The once contemplative students speckled among empty rows turned into a muttering horde of strangers—watching, staring, gaping. The candles flung colossal shadows on the walls. This was not the mission church where I went to seek peace. This was a chamber that echoed *water...Water...WATER*. In my ice blue leotard, I transitioned from shaking uncontrollably to being wholly unable to move.

I don't remember how I finished the piece, but I can still see the senior dance major glaring at me for ruining her choreography.

In the refuge of my bedroom that night, I carved into my journal: *"Wade" was not performing. This was different from stage fright. This is not the way. I cannot force myself—I AM NOT READY.*

I stopped going to the mission church. I stopped going to my dance clubs. My bed became my safe place, my haven from urban life and crowds of strangers.

In poetry class, my professor had mentioned a poet who used not a penname, but what he called an "artist name." On my paisley comforter, I wondered what mine would be. I'd been meeting students with ethnic names they hadn't translated into American "equivalents." I thought of my own ethnic name: $Δήμητρα$, the feminine form of Demetrios, defender of Thessaloniki. After contemplating the Orthodox tradition of saint names, I delved into the core of the word. Delta is the mathematical symbol for change, as in $y_2 - y_1 = Δy$. Change passes from one state to another—from water to solid, from weakness to strength. It signals transformation. In ancient Greek, Demetra is derived from Demeter, goddess of the harvest. Demeter transforms seed into sustenance. Deme comes from the word for village, as opposed to city, or polis. In dance, demi is French for half, as in demi-plié. Half, middle, median. Balance.

I found the name I always had: Demetra Perros.

I began calling myself Deme. The name became a kind of mantra, an affirmation that reminded me to pursue a balanced path. I asked my housemates if they could start calling me Deme. I wanted to see how willing people were to call me by my Greek name. Gratefully, they obliged. When I heard my name, I didn't see the Jamie who returned to high school empty and alone. The sound of Deme brought newness. It sparked an image of myself in the present moment.

My housemate's friend introduced me to the film *Garden State*. The dialogue spoken by Natalie Portman's character taught me something about the balance between seriousness and lightness, about simply being able to laugh at your situation. Seriousness leaves little room for humility, forgiveness, or even joy.

Phone calls from Nick also helped me keep life in perspective. He told me a story about a Sasquatch festival he'd gone to at a bar outside of Elliston, Montana. Every year, a man dressed up in a hairy costume and tromped into the woods. After giving him a head start, the festivalgoers—i.e., bearded, flannel-wearing Montanans—ran into the woods to find him.

"I ended up in a camper," Nick said. "A woman in her sixties was sitting at the table taking shots. Of whiskey. They gave me a lift back to Helena. It was like being on the moon."

Nick told me that in life, there are extremes of seriousness or a lack thereof. I took his Bigfoot camper story to be one extreme, and the pressure I put on myself as another. "I'm not sayin' do the kind of shit my friends and I do, but do get out there." He paused. "So, how's California?"

"I don't...um...feel like I'm in the right place," I said.

"But I thought you wanted to study theatre."

"I did—I just..." I debated with myself about telling Nick more. He didn't know I'd been diagnosed with PTSD. I had been keeping that information private, even from my family members. Mom and Dad knew, but we didn't discuss my therapy.

"You can do whatever you want," Nick said. "You know that, don't you?"

I didn't answer.

Nick recommended I watch *Friday Night Lights*, a film about a Texas high school football team and a star player, number 45, who tears his ACL his senior year. I wrote the title in the margin of my journal and told him I'd rent it.

After watching the film straight through, I played it again with subtitles, pausing every few minutes to scribble dialogue into my journal. Toward the beginning of the film, the head coach tells the quarterback, "You gotta accept the fact that people have to take care of themselves, and that includes you....The truth is, against some pretty overwhelming odds...if you do decide to accept that, you're gonna seriously fly, son."

I pieced together the coach's message: *Against some pretty overwhelming odds*—an adverse drug reaction, posttraumatic stress disorder, chronic gastrointestinal symptoms—I still had the potential to *fly. People have to take care of themselves*, I wrote, *and that includes* me.

It was time.

Time to let go of the struggle. Time to stop feeling ashamed for falling ill on the ship. Time to accept that what had happened was, in fact, beyond my control. Time to grant myself permission to heal, to take care of myself, to start enjoying life.

I was tired of repeatedly adapting to new environments and wrestling with PTSD, and I had discovered that a city was a terrible place for someone trying to recover from trauma. Instead of punishing myself, I worked with this knowledge. I made a decision to return to the familiar.

On my walk home from class one afternoon in March, I called the registrar's office at my former school in Oregon and asked how I could reapply. The process was exceedingly simple. I took that as a sign. The registrar staff didn't ask why I had left in the first place. They didn't take offense as the administration had done at my high school. The only question I was asked was this: "What's your major?"

Pausing on the grass, I consulted my heart, which longed for connections; my mind, which told me it needed a predictable environment; my body, which pleaded for a gentle path; and my soul, which asked for enlightenment. I thought of the objects I'd brought with me to California: dog-eared novels, short story anthologies, journals filled with quotes from authors and poets and screenwriters.

I smiled. "English literature."

Looking back, I would describe being in California as my thawing period. My mind was starting to loosen its rigid hold over my heart, my emotional self was beginning to reconnect, my body was discovering its own voice and asserting its own needs, and my spirit was lifting. Deciding to transfer back to school in Oregon was the first decision I made post-ship where I consulted all four of my "sisters," as Irene called them. Being united in head, heart, body, and soul was a huge victory in the battle with PTSD. Sometimes, when I try to explain why I left, I think that all people hear is that I was too afraid to pursue my passions, too afraid to dance and act. Yes. I was afraid. Not long after leaving California, I would meet another artist who, post-trauma, was afraid of her craft.

ΓΙΙΙ

I am not a coward but a brave woman. I go with you, willingly.

~Euripides, *Hekebe*

When I returned to college in Oregon, my friends—the ones I had left to pursue theatre—welcomed me back with open arms. Literally. I received so many hugs the first month back at school. The hugs, more than anything else, reassured me that I'd been reaccepted into this community. Samantha, my friend from high school, still lived in the same dorm building from our freshman year. Ruby was studying abroad, so Samantha acquired a new roommate named Jae, a first-generation Korean American. I lived a floor above them with an international student named Yukari. Fulfilling my plan to major in English, I enrolled in Shakespearean tragedies, Romantic poetry, and a course on William Faulkner. I also took ancient Greek to begin a minor in classical studies.

Though the university didn't have a dance department, I discovered a way to continue dancing: the cheer team. Cheerleading was a student club that performed at football and basketball games. Because we weren't funded by the university, we couldn't afford liability insurance to perform stunts, so we relied on dance routines, cheers, and our mascot to enliven crowds. The student government on campus allocated money to student clubs. We applied for funding to cover the cost of rain gear, an obvious necessity in the Pacific Northwest, but the Harry Potter club received more than we did. Fuming, we sold soggy brownies to raise enough money for waterproof jackets and wind pants.

At cheer practice, that sense of camaraderie I used to feel at Grandstreet Theatre renewed. There were twelve girls on the cheer team, co-captained by two seniors. They choreographed our routines and told us that if we had any ideas for cheers or dances, we could teach the team. I'd never choreographed a dance before, but just having it as a possibility was enough for me to know that I was in a creative, collaborative environment.

My body felt whole once more. The scar tissue from my incisions was not as sensitive as it had been in California simply because I had given myself the space and time to heal. The precise technique in cheer gave my mind something concrete to hold onto. Unlike the flowy, inexact movements of liturgical dancing, cheer positions were visible and straightforward. We stood in a confident posture, chin up, hitting our positions—big T, little t, high V, low V—as a unit. Standing out was not the objective in cheer. Blending in was. I didn't have to worry about performing a solo. I was part of a matching team, which felt safe yet exhilarating.

That fall, the football team had four home games. I performed at three. A few weeks before the fourth game, I woke up with a sore throat. Instead of walking to the gym for cheer practice, I crunched through fallen leaves to the campus health center. Impatiently, I followed a nurse into the exam room. She drew my blood and told me she'd call with results.

A few days later, my cell phone rang. The nurse said I needed to come in. Again, instead of going to cheer practice, I walked to the campus health center.

"Your blood tests came back," she told me as I checked the time. "Your lab work indicates you have mono with hepatitis."

I listened, trying to hear above the ceaseless ticks of my watch.

"Mononucleosis is contracted by saliva," the nurse explained, "and hepatitis means 'inflammation of the liver.' In most people, the virus is limited to the spleen. But since you don't have a gallbladder, your liver is more vulnerable to infection. Avoid physical activities, and rest as much as you can."

After I left, I slumped down on the steps outside the clinic, my white cheer sneakers turning brown in the wet muck. I stared at my muddy shoes, defeated. I'd just recovered from gallbladder surgery enough to dance again, and now this? Another biological siege intercepting my ability to perform.

Mono waged war on my immune system for three months, during which I refused to drop any classes. I don't remember writing about nature imagery in Shakespeare's tragedies, or Lena Grove in *Light in August*, or heliotropic sunflowers in William Blake's poetry, but apparently I did. When I wasn't sleeping or writing surprisingly coherent papers in my dorm room, I was memorizing ancient Greek words and trying to translate *Frogs* by Aristofanes.

One afternoon, I woke up to an industrial-sized crate of water bottles in the center of the floor. My roommate turned from her computer to look at me.

"Yukari!"

She brushed her bangs away from her eyes and smiled.

"How did you get this up the stairs?"

She shrugged. "I got you melons." She walked over to our mini fridge and held up a gallon-sized bag of cantaloupe and honeydew from the cafeteria. I wanted to hug her but didn't want her to get sick. I also wanted to hug Samantha and Jae, who brought a bowl of rice up to me three times a day.

We concluded that I'd gotten mono from playing beer pong at a party.

Looking back, having mono was one of those typical college experiences. If I could only choose one word to describe the illness, I'd choose *awful*. If I could choose two, *awesomely awful*. What twenty-one-year-old doesn't love sleeping? I became a professional sleeper. A sleep master. I can look back now and laugh, but at the time, I wasn't tired just from the virus. I was tired of the reoccurring pattern of health/sickness, health/sickness, health/sickness. When would it end?

Once a week, I visited my professors. Their offices were located in Beckham Hall, a sprawling brick building blanketed in ivy and moss. Walking from my dorm to Beckham usually took three minutes, but with mono, more like fifteen. Wearing pajamas and a raincoat, I walked through the quad with a hand on my stomach, pausing every few yards to focus beyond the fatigue.

My Shakespeare and Romantic poetry professors were a married couple named Moira and Bernard. Moira was what Ruby called "a force of nature." Her husband was a peaceful man who practiced tai chi and wrote his lesson plans at a coffee shop downtown. Moira and Bernard shared an office, so I met with both of them for my weekly check-ins. One afternoon, I climbed the flight of stairs and collapsed into a loveseat in their office to wait for them. Trying not to fall asleep, I stared at a painting of koi fish behind Bernard's desk until my eyes blurred with hot tears. Moira entered first.

"What's wrong?" she asked.

My head fell into my hands. "All I ever am is sick." My esophagus burned, my stomach ached, and my shirt stuck to my sweaty back.

"Hey," she said. "Life is suffering. But you know what? You have an imagination in you. So use it."

I nodded, hardly comprehending what she meant.

By Christmas break, I was starting to feel better. Samantha and I drove the twelve-hour road trip to Montana together—well, she drove. I slept. When we arrived in Helena, I rested for a few days at Mom's house, until Marika flew home from graduate school.

"Get dressed. We're going downtown." I sat up in my bed and watched my older sister rummage through the makeup on my dresser. "Ohhh," she said, opening a palette of eye shadow. "Can I use this?"

"You'll get mono," I joked.

She looked at me as though I might be serious. "Did you lick it?"

"Yes."

She grabbed a brush and began applying silver to her eyelids.

"Where are you going?" I asked.

"*We're* meeting Gracie Facie for lunch."

Grace and Marika used to play basketball together in middle school. I remember watching their games, admiring Grace's side ponytail and pink scrunchies. When Grace was in high school, my dad hired her to work the hotdog cart in the summers. I used to walk downtown to hang out with her, fetching cans of pop from the cooler or trotting back to Coney Island to get her more hotdog buns when she ran out.

The last time I'd seen Grace was when Marika and I met her for lunch at a golf course in Helena. At the time, I was in eighth grade, and they were sophomores in college. Marika was studying psychology in Washington, and Grace was in Los Angeles majoring in creative writing and minoring in sculpture. Grace walked into the clubhouse wearing a funky pair of sunglasses with yellow lenses. "I should've gotten the pink ones," she said, taking them off.

"They're *cool*," I said, hoping I sounded cool too. I don't remember much about our lunch, just that I sat there taking in Grace's sparkly eyes and bleach blonde hair, her fashionable sunglasses and turquoise sweater.

This time, we met Grace at a sandwich shop a block down the hill from Grandstreet, just off of Last Chance Gulch. She arrived with her older brother. The four of us sat at a table in front of the windows. Across the street, the Montana Club was barely visible through the falling snow. Sometimes Grandstreet held its summer camp dances in the Montana Club's basement bar. One year at camp, Luke and I were scolded there for dancing too close.

I don't recall how the topic came up, but all of a sudden we were talking about Lariam. "I was on it for three months," Grace said. "It was horrible."

My elbow slipped off the table.

"*I thought you might want to come,*" Marika whispered to me.

When Grace was a junior in college, she was prescribed Lariam before taking a language immersion course in Guatemala. She took the drug as directed: two weeks before traveling there, for the duration of her six-week Spanish course, and for a month afterward.

"My mom had to fly to Australia to get me."

"Australia?" I asked.

"After Guatemala, I went to Australia for a semester abroad, during my spring semester."

"What year?" I asked.

"2001." One year after we had lunch with her at the golf course, and three years before my own episode.

"Lariam was created by the Army," Grace's brother explained, "for two-hundred-and-twenty-pound guys." Grace was about my size: a short, petite build. Before she and her brother brought it up, I hadn't considered the drug's origin.

I learned later that the US Army launched a wide scale anti-malarial discovery program in the 1960s and 1970s because of the alarming number of soldiers returning from the Vietnam War with malaria. Funded by the federal government, the Experimental Therapeutics Division of the Walter Reed Army Institute of Research (WRAIR) tested over 250,000 possible drug compounds to combat chloroquine-resistant malaria. Experimental number WR 142,490, later generically named mefloquine and brand named Lariam, was one of the drug compounds chosen to be marketed. WRAIR collaborated with F. Hoffmann-La Roche, a multinational drug company, to market the new drug commercially.

Lariam was quickly approved by the Food and Drug Administration in 1989. Before its FDA approval, Lariam was tested on prisoners at Illinois' Joliet Correction Center and at the Maryland House of Correction. Dr. Ashley Croft, a public health consultant at the Medical Branch of Headquarters 5th Division in Shrewsbury, UK, explains that no randomized trials were conducted "in a normal study population of healthy civilian volunteers" before Lariam became commercialized. He also points out that "there was no serious attempt prior to licensing to explore the potential drug–drug interactions." This limited research contributed to what he calls a "gap in the prescribers' knowledge base." Health care professionals were not equipped to identify reactions or side effects because the drug was barely studied before going on the market.

"Belatedly," Croft informs, "three randomized controlled trials were carried out in healthy volunteer populations, and were reported between 2001–2003....[A]ll three study reports described an excess of neuropsychiatric adverse effects in the mefloquine arm." Mefloquine was also found to be neurotoxic. In other words, it poisons the brain.

"I was diagnosed with bipolar disorder," Grace said.

I stopped chewing my sandwich.

"In Australia," she said. "When they locked me up."

Her brother pushed his empty basket aside. "She was misdiagnosed for five years," he said. "Five. *Years*."

"How'd you find out it was Lariam?" I asked.

"Our aunt," her brother said.

"She's a nurse up in Great Falls," Grace explained. "A friend of hers had just returned from traveling abroad. Her symptoms sounded a lot like mine. Our aunt asked for my medical records. We did research. Put two and two together."

"Did you vomit? Have a rash? Gallbladder problems?"

"No, just a lot of..." she folded her napkin, "psychological issues."

"Paranoia?" I asked.

She nodded, but didn't make eye contact with anyone.

"Hallucinations?"

She nodded again, still looking at her napkin.

"Me too."

Her eyes met mine.

Marika leaned in, as if expecting me to disclose my own experience. I didn't. I just watched Grace, not feeling a distance in age anymore. It was like seeing a character I knew I could play. But this was not a play; this was someone's life. I noticed the oversized orange purse with fringe tassels Grace had placed on the table, the silver jacket on the back of her chair, and a green pendant around her neck. What I saw wasn't just a stylish wardrobe you couldn't find in Montana. I saw an artist attempting to express her creative self, but in a safe, controlled way, in containable pieces of flair that could be neatly tucked into a closet at the end of the day.

"Do you still write?" I asked her. "Or sculpt?"

"No."

A week later, I met Grace at the same sandwich shop before she flew back to LA and I returned to Oregon. We ordered smoothies and sat at the same table as before.

"I got you something," I said, reaching into my bag. "It's helping me. I thought maybe it'd help you too." I set a book on the table: *The Artist's Way*, by Julia Cameron. It was a how-to on recovering one's creative self. Many of the exercises utilized writing—writing out your fears until they no longer suppressed your desire to create. My mother had bought the book for me as a high school graduation present, but I didn't begin to use it until I was in California.

"Thank you," she said.

"Have you heard of it?"

"I have." She sipped her smoothie. "Someone else recommended I try it." A note in her voice made me realize the book hadn't worked for her. "Thank you," she said again, tucking the book into her orange purse.

I smiled, hoping my face didn't betray my disappointment. Maybe I was wrong to assume she'd want to recover her sense of creativity. Maybe she was satisfied with not writing or sculpting anymore. But I wasn't satisfied with that. I had to believe in Grace. I had to believe that she, like I, could find comfort in art once more.

We finished our smoothies and bundled up to face the cold. She told me to call her if I ever needed to talk. Wishing I hadn't given her the book, I hugged her and said I would.

Six years later, Grace told me more about her experience on Lariam. I was writing my graduate thesis and wanted the personal story of another artist who'd taken the drug. We arranged a phone interview: she talking, me typing her words.

She said that while she was in Guatemala, she began to notice that her mind was "very free." At the time, she was studying magical realism, a genre of fiction that integrates fantastical elements into the real world. She believed she was achieving what her literature professors had been talking about. "I was extremely open to the idea of the dream world following me throughout the day," she said. "I let my mind go where it wanted. I felt as though I was experiencing life more intensely. My senses were really strong. I ate a grapefruit one day and thought, *Whoa! This is the best grapefruit ever!* I attributed it to being in a new environment—the fruit, the rain forest, this tropical climate."

After her six-week program in Guatemala, she visited her family in Helena for two weeks, then crossed the international date line to Australia, where she took her last two weekly doses of Lariam.

The first week she arrived in Australia, the university kept changing her class schedule. "When I finally got the updated version, I couldn't read it. I went to my adviser and asked her what it said. Now, I'd always done really well on tests. But all of a sudden, I couldn't read." She laughed and told me that when she did go to class, she attended the wrong ones.

"Ever since I was a kid," she said, "I've had this ability to wake up without my alarm clock. I just know when it's time to get up. But in Australia, my sense of time was all messed up. I kept missing my classes. And I didn't have the ability to follow through on activities. I got my period in Australia but didn't know where to buy tampons. Now, I'd traveled around the world before—I'd lived in LA—I could find my way around. But going to a store didn't cross my mind. In the dorm bathroom, a new tampon was on the countertop. I thought someone had left it there for me because they knew I needed one. So I didn't buy any. I got it in my head that I could control the flow." She laughed. "To think that I was able to somehow control the flow. That would never occur to me in my normal frame of mind. Weird, right?"

"Not on Lariam," I told her.

"Did you have thoughts like that?" Grace asked.

"I started my period too," I said, "on the ship. I remember it starting, but I have no idea what became of it—if I took care of it or not. When I saw the blood, I remember thinking, *Oh, my body sent protection. It's protecting me.*"

"That sounds perfectly normal to me," she joked. "So, the period thing was only the borderline of weirdness. I was trying to figure out the world. That film, *A Beautiful Mind*, totally made sense to me. I couldn't read, but I saw codes and patterns to help me make sense of the world. I looked for messages in newspaper funnies. *This means something*, I thought. *Someone is communicating something to me.* A phone number flashed across the TV screen. I didn't see it as a phone number, but as a code for something else.

"I remember people implying that I was starting to lose it, or testing me to see if I was. At a barbeque, a guy made a joke in front of me about spies on rooftops. I didn't react. I didn't give him what he wanted to hear.

"What else...it's all kind of a big jumble. I have this really weird memory of a word painted on a tree. My mom's or my grandma's maiden name. In red. It meant something. I don't think there really was a word painted on the tree. I think some things I was seeing might not have been there. Not obvious things, just little details that wouldn't make sense in the real world."

"But that would've made sense in, say, a story by Gabriel Garcia Marquez," I said.

"Yeah, exactly," said Grace. "I started having bizarre dreams in Guatemala. I had one about a naked ape-man standing outside my room, watching me. That was an intense dream that really made an impact on my mind. It was hard to tell if I was dreaming or awake or what was going on."

One severe psychiatric side effect of mefloquine is hallucinations. Dr. Alan Stoudemire of Emory University defines hallucinations as "perceptions that occur in the absence of actual stimuli." When individuals have hallucinations, they are unaware that what they are experiencing is not real. Whether or not an ape-man was actually standing outside Grace's room makes no difference to how her body responded. The emotional and physical impact of the perceived event is *the same* as how she would respond to actually being stalked. In that moment, she *was* being stalked. Even afterward, when the event has been identified as a hallucination, the physiological impact cannot be reversed.

"I was afraid to sleep with the door shut," Grace said about her dorm room in Australia. "I had this idea that I'd be safer with the door cracked open, so I could hear someone approaching. I've had a hard time sleeping since I was little, which started when my parents got divorced, when I was twelve. I'd go on runs at five in the morning, which was never a problem in Helena. When I went to Australia, I went for walks early, *early* in the morning. A man picked me up and took me to his office. He called my school. Returned me to the dorms. That following Monday, the psych ward people showed up to take me away. They were wearing these big orange suits. They put me in a dogcatcher mobile—you know, like that vehicle in Helena that picks up stray dogs.

"They asked if I was on drugs. The way I understood it—and the way they said it—I thought they meant street drugs. They didn't find the bottle of Lariam in my room. I had already finished the last dose. This was the third week in Australia. The fourth week I spent in the psych ward."

On the *Interlude*, the ship nurse asked me a similar question: "Are you taking any medications?" I told her no. The way she worded the question, and the way I interpreted it, was that she was asking if I was on any medications for an established illness like asthma or diabetes. In my mind, an antimalarial didn't fall into that category. It was like a vaccine, different from a medication. Of course, Oceans Abroad had my medical records and the information that stated what vaccines I had received prior to boarding and which antimalarial I was currently taking.

"I was placed in a suite with a woman in her forties," Grace continued. "One day, she went into the bathroom and broke the mirror. She came out with a huge piece in her hand and threatened to kill me.

"I was diagnosed with bipolar disorder. They gave me all these shots and medications. I refused at first. I'd met a man who was taking one of the same meds they wanted to give me. The man had developed a facial tic from the drug—a long-term side effect. 'I'm not taking it,' I decided. So they tranquilized me. Six people pinned me to the floor. They pulled down my pants. Gave me the shot.

"Then I was locked in a padded room with no windows. There was no light in that room. I still can't sleep in a room that's dark. I don't need an actual nightlight, but light from a street lamp works, just something to help orient where I am. Once, back in California, I woke up to pitch blackness. It was horrifying—I thought I was still in the psych ward."

When Grace finally left Australia, two pieces of information stayed with her: "I was crazy, and that at any moment, I'd have another episode. I was really afraid of the diagnosis. When I got back to Helena, my parents set up appointments. The therapists I saw didn't think I was bipolar. The psych ward had given me the diagnosis after one day, but usually people are monitored for much longer before being diagnosed. I went to therapy for four years. My therapist said that I most likely didn't have bipolar disorder, but that maybe I had 'magical thinking,' which is probably the closest thing to being on Lariam.

"Five years after Australia, my aunt called me up and told me about her friend who had a similar experience. It all lined up amazingly well. Before that, there hadn't been any explanation. Only that I was crazy, and that it'd happen again. I continued reading about other people's experiences on mefloquine and how they paralleled my own."

Grace told me that when she came back from Australia, she took a semester off, then returned to Los Angeles to finish her last semester of college. She had two more classes required in the arts, but she found them almost impossible to complete. "Doing anything—engaging in any activity that encouraged me to be creative was...*fear.* I would call it fear. Anything that made it difficult to distinguish between the dream world and reality scared me. I couldn't identify the differences all the time—what was real, what wasn't. I would not consider allowing my mind to be that free again. Before, I would've welcomed that. But now, there's this cage around my mind."

The fear I had felt onstage in California was similar to Grace's sense of fear. While the limitations I experienced were related more to my body and hers to her mind, both of our mediums of expression had been compromised.

"When I was taken to the psych ward," Grace said, "an official at the Australian university went through my dorm room. All my personal stuff. I was keeping a journal—I wanted to be a writer, that's what you do. I had written some poetry in there. While I was in the hospital trying to get the nurses to call my parents, the doctors were reading my journal. They were writing notes in the margins—*incoherent thoughts...abstractions...surreal thinking.*

"I didn't write for a long time after that. Only academic papers. I completed one creative writing course afterward, but I didn't enjoy it. I was scared of it, that my writing could be used against me. I had been taught by my professors that being unique and having your own style was good. Then, being unique was bad. People could use that to judge me. They could look at my outpouring of thoughts and think I was crazy. That scene changed my life. The level of art I did—written, sculpture—I don't think I could ever reach that again. Even though at one point that was a dream of mine. The long-term impact of my experience," Grace said, "is directly related to the process of art."

This time, at twenty-seven, I didn't have the urge to give her books on how to recover her creative self. She had recovered her *self.* Period. But Grace's sense of self, like mine, has taken years to rebuild.

"I was emotionally devastated by Australia," she said. "Afterward, I had a severe lack of confidence. I was scared of everything. Up until Australia, my life had been pretty easy. I had a lot of doors and options open to me, but not afterward. Going back to school, and having the confidence to pursue any type of career path, was very difficult. I had wanted to be an artist. Then I didn't. I didn't know what I wanted to be. After college, I came upon occupational therapy, so I started taking prerequisites for that. I started going out more, but I was afraid of what would happen if I didn't get enough sleep. Even after I found out that my episode had been caused by Lariam, I was still concerned. I wanted to go to graduate school but didn't know if I could manage the responsibility."

Eventually, Grace was accepted into a doctoral program in occupational therapy. She wrote her dissertation about the homecoming phase of veterans returning from combat zones. To help veterans overcome symptoms of PTSD, she designed a doctoral project that utilized extreme sports like rock climbing and mountain biking to provide an alternate form of therapy.

"I believe that any support you provide for someone with PTSD," Grace said, "should have a physical component. Counseling is important, but I think you need more than that."

"Like dance," I said.

"Yes. Any physical activity that puts you into safe, controlled situations, where your body is responding constructively to that fear mode. Oddly enough," she said with a laugh, "occupational therapy *is* creative."

ΓΙΙΙ

Through this shall I endure.
~Euripides, *Ifigeneia in Aulis*

The winter after having mono, I returned to campus in Oregon and contracted norovirus. The illness had been spreading across the nation that season, and with my mono-weakened immune system, I was an easy target. The abdominal cramps and watery diarrhea I experienced were comparable to the GI upset I had my freshman year of college. My parents urged me to find a GI specialist off campus, but I resisted. Doctor visits triggered those old feelings of invalidation and anger, feelings I wanted to avoid. With norovirus, nausea tempted my throat, but I swallowed the urge to vomit. Since recovering from Oceans Abroad, I had vomited once, when I was given a painkiller after gallbladder surgery. I wanted to keep that number low because I was afraid vomiting might catapult me back onto the ship.

Inevitably, I was catapulted back to the ship. After having mono, ironically, I stopped being able to fall asleep. Lack of sleep intensified my PTSD symptoms. Suddenly, scenes were appearing that I hadn't been able to access before: snorkeling in the Philippines, the smell of peppermint gum, getting my passport stamped at Heathrow, the taste of bile, doing push-ups on the deck. As the three-year anniversary approached, a spliced film reel kept playing through my mind. I felt ambivalent about these images. I only had a handful of memories from Oceans Abroad. Sometimes I tried to bat them away; other times I held them with a vice grip because they were all I had. I wanted to pause, rewind, zoom in, speed up, tear the ribbon out of the video tape.

One afternoon, Samantha knocked quietly on my door.

"Come in," I called from under the covers. I had been living in my bed for what felt like forever. Samantha sat on my comforter and checked the temperature of my forehead. "You should wash your hands," I told her.

"Nah, I won't get sick." She set a container from the cafeteria on my nightstand. "We haven't yet, have we?" she asked, referring to her and Jae's continuous pre-med nurturing.

"I'm sick and tired of being sick and tired."

"You've fought through worse," Samantha said.

"I'm tired of fighting."

I stared at a film poster of *The Two Towers* on the wall opposite my bed. Samantha followed my gaze. "Remember in high school," she said, "when we went to the midnight opening?"

"And we were still wearing our choir dresses?"

She sniggered.

"I won't be able to graduate with you guys," I said. "I had to drop my morning class because I couldn't get up in time. Pathetic, I know." Because I had taken time off after my freshman year and attended school in California for only one quarter, I was behind on trying to graduate college in four years. Life, I would reluctantly grow to accept, doesn't happen in neat four-year plans.

Samantha checked to see if I'd eaten the bowl of rice Jae had left me. "I'll stop by again after bio," she said.

"Thank you." *For everything*, I wanted to say. *For our entire history together—supporting me pre- and post-ship at high school, helping me through freshman year in Oregon, not being hurt when I transferred to California, being happy to see me when I transferred back.*

"Please," she scoffed. "I bring you applesauce and toast."

"You've done more than just feed me."

She didn't say, *I know*. Instead, she handed me the container from the cafeteria. "Get your shit together," she said. "Literally."

A week or so later, I finally saw a GI specialist. His clinic was just off campus. The doctor entered the exam room and introduced himself. He looked in his early forties, groomed beard, light hair. He asked a series of questions about my health history. I didn't tell him I had posttraumatic stress disorder, but I did ask him if trauma affects the GI tract.

"Any trauma," he said, "can affect the digestive system. Even giving birth is a trauma to the body. People can have different bowel habits during and after pregnancy."

I wasn't planning on making babies anytime soon, but hearing that something as common as pregnancy could alter one's bowels made me feel a little better. The doctor didn't pry, didn't ask why I brought up the topic. He asked me how I was sleeping, a question I wasn't asked by any provider post-ship.

"I'm not sleeping well at all," I answered. "When I finally do fall asleep, it's hard to wake up in the morning."

"Something happens when we reach the deep sleep cycle," he said, "that is very important for our digestive system."

"What is it?" I asked.

"We don't really know. It's something—like a rebooting—that helps our GI tract stay healthy. We actually don't know a whole lot about the digestive system."

A gastroenterologist, who had at least a decade of formal medical education and training behind him, had just admitted to me that the GI system was enigmatic. He seemed awed by the body, respectful of what we cannot know fully.

A smile spread across my face. My breathing relaxed.

He prescribed a medication to help me reach the deep sleep cycle. "I'm recommending a low dose," the doctor said. "It'll also help manage your chronic abdominal pain."

I kept smiling, my digestive pain finally acknowledged.

"This medication, traditionally, is an antidepressant."

My cheeks dropped into a frown.

"Like the brain," he explained, "the GI tract has its own nervous system. This drug targets pain receptors in the gut. Treating depression requires a much higher dose. I tell my patients this because sometimes they are uneasy about starting it."

I was uneasy. But I reminded myself that this doctor wasn't a psychiatrist; he was a gastroenterologist. I trusted that he was addressing my bowel pain, not indirectly trying to "cure" my mind with a pill. Since my adverse reaction to mefloquine, however, I was wary of taking any form of medication, antimalarial or not. After I returned from the ship, I tore through my mom's house, throwing away bottles of pills, convinced they, like Lariam, had the potential to mess up my life.

"What if I become dependent on this drug?" I asked the GI specialist. "What if it's enabling?"

"Is taking a pill once a night," he asked, "any worse than how you're doing now?"

I thought about this line of reasoning. Was staying up all night combatting flashbacks and cramping up before every bowel movement better for me than taking one pill once a day?

"What side effects does it have?"

He told me that the drug had been on the market for decades. "Cottonmouth and morning drowsiness are the most common side effects." He handed me the prescription. "Think about it more, and if or when you're ready, you can get it filled."

I should've gotten it filled right after the appointment.

Instead, I deliberated.

Between being bedridden from mono and norovirus, and being unable to cheer at basketball games, I had acquired a lot of pent up energy. So, holed up in my dorm room, I began watching grand scale films: *The Fellowship of the Ring, The Two Towers, Gladiator, Troy, 300.* After I finished my course papers and readings, I transcribed epic war speeches. Or, at other times, a single line:

THIS IS SPARTAAAAA!

Such satisfaction I felt, such drum beats.

Renewing my Greek heritage, I launched myself into classical studies research. Using my imagination, I fashioned a Korinthian helmet, pondered bronze welding, wove a snaky aegis—an apotropaic breastplate made of Medusa's pelt. I also got really into *Macbeth*, and *Hamlet*, and NFL football.

One weekend in February, I surveyed my dorm room: clean laundry hanging in the closet, a presentation outline about the oracle in Delfi on my desk, stacks of ancient tragedies dog-eared and fanned with sticky notes. I frowned at the document on my computer screen: a stream of quotes from *The Fellowship of the Ring*. How had I digressed from calling cheers at football games to transcribing riddles by Bilbo Baggins? I missed it, all of it. Performing. The sweat and discipline. The camaraderie, being part of something greater, merging into that universal energy, that transcendent uplift. I had not felt anything that *moved* me for so long. My lament was the artist's— an actor stripped of stage, a singer of voice, a dancer of wood floor. Middle-earth could sustain me for only so long.

With spring break approaching, I had two choices: stay on campus and sink deeper into the intangible triumphs of epic war heroes, or go home to my own Myrmidon.

The night I flew back to Montana for spring break, Nick and I were sitting in his truck eating gyros, our wrappers dripping with tzatziki sauce and olive oil. "So, how's life?" he asked, chunks of feta falling from his face. "You look small."

I felt small, insignificant. Resisting an urge to cry, I bit into the gyro meat. "Well," I said thickly, "I've lost a lot of muscle mass. Mono really pillaged me, you know."

He knew. I'd call him after every cheer practice, frustrated by my inability to dance the high-impact, rigid motions, yearning for an escape into his landscape and irrigation stories.

"How're you doing, really?"

I tried to communicate the welter beneath my stoic facade, but didn't know where to start. I still hadn't told my brother about my battle with PTSD. I didn't want him to think any differently of me. Any less of me. "Something," I told Nick, "is taking hold. Something tracing back to...the ship. I don't know what triggered it. Nothing. Everything. My lack of sleep. The lights in the library. The basement of my dorm building. Everything reminds me of being trapped below deck." Dry heaving, hallucinating, paranoid, emaciated. Flashbacks left me panicked on the stark bathroom floor, wrapped in a chilled ball of sweatpants and hoodie. They kept me from classical studies classes, Faulkner seminars, lunchtime. Acid reflux corroded my chest. Lower abdominal pain doubled me over at cheer practice. "I can't dance, can't sleep, can't—I can't look at telephone poles without seeing the masts and rigging. At night, I can feel the *Interlude* docked right outside my window."

Cursing a tear for streaking my cheekbone, I glanced over at Nick, wondering if he had followed my lurching story. His eyes—they were welling, shining in the streetlight that seeped through the tinted windows. I watched a crease of lightning pierce his forehead and his black eyelashes dampen. My face sank into his chest. His hoplite hand patted what must've been his little sister's perfect mind.

After spring break, I asked Samantha if she could walk with me to the pharmacy off campus. Enabling or not, I was ready to give the medication a try. I started slowly on the drug: half a pill for a week as instructed, then three-quarters, then a full dose. Samantha gave me a pair of hot pink ear plugs, telling me she wore them at night to block out typical dorm noises. I also started wearing a soft sleeping mask. With the ear plugs, the sleeping mask, and the medication, I reached a zero-sensory zone of blackness. I heard nothing and saw nothing, which allowed my mind to relax when I went to bed. Within a month, I was able to sleep through the night without having cognitive attacks.

"No more rice." I set a stack of clean bowls and chopsticks onto Jae's desk. A *Friends* episode was playing on the mini TV in her and Samantha's dorm room. No matter how many times Jae watched the series, Joey always made her crack up.

"Hey, come to hula with me," she said. She combed her sleek hair into a ponytail. "It starts at seven. In the gym studio."

I inventoried my body: mono fatigue gone, norovirus flushed from my system, muscles yearning for action. "I'll grab my water bottle."

Every spring, the university's Hawaii club sponsored a lu'au. Students performed Maori, Tahitian, Samoan, and Hawaiian dances. There were two main styles of hula: the ancient kahiko, and the modern 'auana. The first year I danced, my body gravitated toward the gentler 'auana. The quiet songs and the smoothness in form and movement granted a nurturing alternative to cheerleading. No tight fists and locked knees. No jumping and landing. 'Auana encouraged graceful arms, expressive hands, and a deliberate placement of the feet.

A year later, I finally felt healthy enough to dedicate myself to the more strenuous ancient kahiko. The women's kahiko was led by Leolani, a college student who danced professionally on her home island of Oahu. Leolani brought an intensity to rehearsals that demanded what ancient Greeks would have called αρετή (arete): excellence in mind, body, and spirit. The practices that ensued—the downbeat of the ipu gourd, the memorization of Hawaiian words, the sustained concentration in front of a mirror while our fingertips dove like dolphins—exhilarated me. My body craved the movement. I felt my feet, my bare feet, re-rooting. Grounded. I felt my fingers bloom pua, my arms sculpt the cliffs, my shoulders heave the spear. I heard...my voice. Chanting. There was no monologuing lyrics, no belting. Not even character development. Just emulating. Emulating the Polynesian warriors, similar to ancient Greek heroes, yet with legends that were lusher, more connected to the earth. We thundered their war calls: *'Uwā ka pihe i Pu'umoe'awa.*

"You perpetuate," Leolani lectured, cradling the ipu gourd in her lap. "You channel the fire goddess Pele. Your hair flows like her magma, your eyes blaze like her fire, and your hips hit like her battle drums."

I coveted her war speeches.

"The kahiko," Leolani said, "is the ancient form of hula. It tells the story of our history, our beliefs, and our way of life. Everything in kahiko is symbolic. The earth tone skirts, the braided headpieces, the kukui necklaces. The kahiko is butchered by hotel luʻaus," she threw in, daring someone to object.

We began with what my past theatre directors would call a script analysis of the oli, the chant. It told of the icy Kīpuʻupuʻu rains, which served as a battle metaphor for the twelve hundred runners and spear fighters lent to King Kamehameha I. These fighters raged like the winds to defend their lands.

After studying the oli, we began the dance. Our hands formed the words of the chant, while our feet followed the beat of the drum. Standing in between Jae and Samantha, I mimicked the movements Leolani taught us. Together, we traveled forward in formation, pointed—hela, hela—and whooshed the wind above our heads. Our hālau, our troupe dancers, moved as one: rising like koa trees, spreading like rain, swelling like the surf. We marched to battle like birds tearing into the red petals of lehua flowers.

A few weeks into rehearsals, I gathered the courage to write Leolani an e-mail. Though we were the same age, Leolani was intimidating. Her conviction, strictness, and vast knowledge of Hawaiian culture made her seem almost separate from her peers. Before typing, I debated how much to reveal about my past. *For three years*, I typed, *I punished my body for something that was out of its control. What I feel while dancing hula is something wholly different. The region of my body that received so much negative attention is the core of power in this dance form.* Leolani responded to my e-mail by inviting me to her dorm after rehearsal the next evening.

In her dorm room, Leolani grabbed a hefty binder from a bookcase. Sitting on the floor, she turned each page, showing me newspaper clippings, competition programs, and photographs chronicling her history with hula. The binder reminded me of the old theatre booklet my mother and I had compiled. Leolani was proud to share hers, whereas I had thrown mine out, along with the Oceans Abroad brochures, scholarship letter, and notes Gabe had given me on how to succeed in the interview—every piece of paper that had helped me believe in myself and in my dreams.

Leolani smoothed a crinkled flower that had been pressed between two pages. "Hula is what you need," she said. I nodded, thinking about how much I'd recovered since dancing in the blue leotard at the mission church. "Don't push it," she warned, more instructor-like. "Just sink lower to get your hips matching the front line."

She had placed me in the front line of dancers, a role I finally felt I could fulfill.

In the gym studio one evening, Leolani motioned for us to sit in a circle. "The downbeat of the ipu is called *u*," she instructed. "This sound is made with the heel of the gourd hitting the ground, and the *te*, or upbeat, by tapping the side of the gourd with your hand." Kneeling on an embroidered mat, she demonstrated:

u, te, u, te te

u, te, u, te te

I peered at the double gourd. Its hourglass body curved voluptuously above and below its waist. The ipu was the archetypal goddess, an icon of full-bodied fertility. A deep boom filled the depths of the drum, a vibration that resounded in my chest. I inhaled and exhaled, the fight within me easing. Bronze armor, blazing stage lights, Korinthian helmet, character shoes—they seemed irrelevant now. All hula required was bare feet and a receptive heart. Hula was realigning my senses and washing my spirit. I felt my surgical incisions evaporate from my skin, layer upon layer of scar tissue lift and dissolve. I tasted not metallic triumph, but fresh tranquility. I saw that I was golden without the gilt, my core resilient without the aegis. I was becoming unified, in harmony with the inner and the outer. I was rising once more, a wiser sense of strength grounding my legs yet uplifting my soul. I was reclaiming the artist's body.

I was beating my own war drum.

On the morning of the luʻau, my family met me in the quad. Mom had flown in the previous day. Dad had driven twelve hours from Montana, and he had convinced Johnny, now a senior in high school, to come with him. Spring was in full bloom on campus, sakura blossoms dotting the branches and pink petals blanketing the grass.

"Jamie," Mom said, hugging my waist, "I'm so proud of you."

"Yeah, Jamie, you're gonna rock it," Johnny said.

My family would eventually get used to calling me Deme. Yet I didn't mind hearing them use my childhood name. It reminded me that I was not severed from my teenage self, but rather, that Deme and Jamie were one and the same. The body that fell sick on the ship was the same body that stood here, with my family, ready to perform once more.

We ate sandwiches at a riverfront park a few blocks from campus. All four of us, including my father and mother, sat on a wide bench swapping pickles and chips. My parents weren't bickering as they used to. They were getting along. This luʻau would be the first performance of mine that they were attending, in the same audience, since the opening night of *Barnum*. They were even going to sit at the same table.

"Mom," Johnny said, "didn't you study hula?"

In the sunlight, our mother looked serene, ageless. She told us that she had studied on Oahu for a summer semester in college, thirty-five years ago. When I was little, I used to look through her photo album of Hawaii. In the pictures, she had short curly hair, like now, and a dancer's fit, tan body. "We picked leaves and braided headpieces and anklets before our performances."

"We did that too! After dress rehearsal last night." I glanced at my watch. "I'd better get back to my dorm," I said, not wanting to leave.

"Mom has everyone's tickets. You're sitting to the right of the stage, close, where I'll be dancing." I felt a wash of excitement, then a wave of nerves.

I had given myself two hours to prepare for the luʻau. In my dorm room, I turned on quiet 'auana music, rolled out a spongy yoga mat and stepped onto it, barefoot. My calves felt supple once more, like ripe mangos, my thighs thick like palm trunks, my core hard as waves yet soft as rain. Standing, I placed my arms at chest level and sank my knees into "hula neutral."

In theatre, neutral stance is the powerhouse position. From neutral, you can drop to the ground, rise up on your toes, pivot, lunge. You can find your character, begin your blocking, or start your chore-ography. Hula too has a neutral position, which I realized one night at practice.

"Whatcha doing?" Jae had asked me.

"Just finding hula neutral."

The other dancers looked over at us.

"With acting," I told them, "neutral is the powerhouse stance. You stand parallel, your hips and shoulders square, just like in hula. Your chin is lifted slightly, also like hula. Your hands rest at your sides, wrists relaxed, fingers soft. I've modified it for hula. See?" I bent my elbows and placed my hands in front of my chest. I bent my knees and sank low.

Taking my lead, the dancers mimicked the stance. From it, we vamped with the kāholo step, we slid into a kalākaua, and we flared our knees in a frog-like 'uwehe. As I watched the other dancers mimicking me, my eyes warmed like Pele's embers. I had bridged two worlds, two realms of performance.

It wasn't all confidence all the time. On my yoga mat, an hour before the performance, nervousness was creeping into my pores. I practiced deep breathing to quell this invasion. Lying on my back, I rested a hand on my diaphragm and watched as it rose and fell. I hadn't performed with this much pressure since night mass at the chapel. I didn't know how my body would react. I believed in its capability but had no idea how it would respond to crashing applause, glaring stage lights, and the dark sea beyond.

During dress rehearsal last night, I had imagined the gym bleachers teeming with people, spilling with chatter and chaos. In my panic, I became separated from the hālau, alone on a bare stage with nothing but a trembling body. In the front row, before a thousand invisible eyes, I forgot to kao, kao, kao, 'uwehe. Leolani glared in my direction.

Sitting on the yoga mat, my fingers kneaded the spongy surface. My toes contracted. My stomach tightened. Finally, I inhaled and exhaled slowly. "I am grounded yet uplifted," I said out loud. *Grounded yet uplifted*. My hands found neutral. My mind found peace.

Half an hour before call, I walked to the gym in a floral print dress, or aloha wear, our required attire while greeting guests. Inside the entrance hall of the field house, I spotted my family waiting in a long line for kalua pork. Johnny and Dad were wearing button-down shirts printed with palm trees. "Aloha wear!" I squealed. "Where'd you get these?"

"I packed them," Dad said.

"Amazing!" Something about seeing those two dressed up filled me with such joy. I missed sharing my life with my family. The years following the ship seemed shrouded in silence. Too much silence. My family had respected my request to not talk about it when I had returned. But I wasn't an angsty teen anymore. I was almost twenty-three and still hadn't had an actual conversation about Oceans Abroad with either of my parents. A point is reached when silence contributes to the wound.

Though we rarely talked about our emotions, I was beginning to understand how my family communicated. Flying in, driving seven hundred miles for this one performance, packing aloha wear shirts, and sitting at the same table showed support in ways that words could not. "We have good health insurance," Dad told me a few summers before. "See Irene as much as you need. As much as you need to."

The decorating committee had transformed the auditorium into an island of elephant leaves, plumeria petals, and birds-of-paradise. I

met up with Jae and Samantha in the women's tent, where we changed
into our costumes for the kahiko: coal black skirts, lava red tops, kukui
nut necklaces, and spiky maile leaves crowning our heads.

Marching to our places backstage, I caught a glimpse of the auditorium, the audience, and the lights. My feet stopped. *Grounded yet
uplifted*, I reminded myself. I exhaled my tension and stepped onstage.
Standing proud, hands at our hips, our hālau formed the dance ranks.
We looked individual yet uniform, the perfect balance for a troupe
of dancers. Leolani, kneeling downstage left, chanted and drummed
with her ipu. As one, we listened for our thunderous cue:

TE, TE, U

We pointed our feet, the calm before the storm. Merging with the
Waimea winds, the Kīpuʻupuʻu rains, and the twelve hundred runners
and spear fighters, we danced.

DELTA

Reversals:
the opposite
of what was expected

What I speak furnishes you with feathers.
~Aristofanes, *Birds*

The autumn after discovering hula, I took an art history class on
ancient Greek art and architecture. The course opened with an
overview of the Egyptian Era, then delved into the Minoan Period,
2200–1500 BCE, at the Palace of Knossos on Krete. Narrated by the
gruff voice of our professor, we watched slides of the palace's sophis-
ticated plumbing, quirky frescos, and mysterious double ax symbols.
We learned that archaeologists have been unable to identify a distinct
main entrance or fortification wall enclosing the grounds. Instead,
the site grows organically around a central courtyard in a labyrinth
of turns and dead ends. Did this labyrinthine plan defend the palace
from attack? Or did the inhabitants enjoy peace and therefore need no
defensive walls? Archaeologists are unsure whether Knossos was even
a royal palace or the region's commercial distribution center.

Rather than discourage or disappoint, the uncertainty of art history
ignited my imagination. During lectures, I concentrated on the slides
and built the set around me—a stout column here, the griffin-like
paintings there, stacks of Linear A tablets, dried oregano hanging in
cool storage rooms, pythoi of olive oil—until I reconstructed the site as

it might have been. While the lack of knowledge I'd received about my abdominal attacks and GI symptoms had frustrated and angered me, this was a blissful type of no-knowledge.

As the course progressed, we chronicled the style of faces depicted on statues. In the Archaic Period, sculptures wore the "archaic smile," a forced grin carved into marble. The archaic smile is how I'd describe my outward appearance after my parents divorced, from September of second grade to December of my senior year in high school. That smile solidified into a mask, a mask that told people—and myself—that I wasn't fazed by the fact that home was splitting down the center.

After February 17, 2004, I assumed the face of High Classical sculptures: full cheeks, closed lips, blank eyes. The "stoic" style, the "severe" style, art historians call it. An expressionless face. When Nick was a senior in high school, a single object had changed his life. His football injury affected our entire family. His pain became our pain. His wrenched knee became our knee. My family grieved not with him, but as him. When I returned from Cambodia my own senior year, I didn't want to resurrect that shared experience of hurt and loss we had felt from Nick's injury. My family were not the ones foolish enough to believe they could sail the world on a tall ship. I was, and I refused to let my folly become theirs. So I used my acting skills to veil my hurt, the same skills I'd been honing since third grade at Grand-street Theatre School. I masked, disguised, masked, minimized.

But a face is merely a face.

In my dorm room one evening in October, I was lying on my paisley comforter, flipping through the art history textbook. I passed the Bronze Age, the Geometric Period, the Archaic, Classical, High Classical, until I turned to the Hellenistic Era, a span of time post-Alexander the Great and pre-Roman conquest. I stopped on a page where a winged statue stood alight. Feathers fanned out behind her, a delicate garment clung to her powerful body, and thick drapery swirled around her muscular thighs. *Nike of Samothrace*, I read, *the winged goddess of victory*. Something about the statue moved me, so I dedicated the next several weeks to researching the goddess.

Nike would appear on battlefields or at the end of athletic events to crown the victorious. She also rewarded victors at poetry competitions and other literary festivals. Nearly every depiction of Nike in ancient Greek art is portrayed with wings because victory is fleeting, an ephemeral moment that cannot be captured and caged. Neither flying nor landing, she exists between the divine and mortal world. In the Hellenistic Era, sculptors finally began portraying pathos, or suffering and emotion. Faces betrayed the anguish of dying Gauls, the timid surprise of a crouching Afrodite, the resignation of aged athletes, and the scarred brow and cauliflower ears of a weary boxer long forgotten by the victory goddess.

Made of Parian marble, Nike of Samothraki stands eight feet tall, with a six-foot wingspan. She lunges in a striking "K" pose on a marble pediment shaped like the prow of a fighting ship. Dated around 190 BCE, the victory goddess commemorated a naval triumph of some kind. She may have been dedicated by the island of Rhodes after their victory over Antioxos III, or commissioned by naval general Demetrios Poliorketes after a Makedonian victory at Salamis. Some archaeologists say she had been visible from the sea, while others say she overlooked an amphitheatre, placed in a fountain imitating waves and sea spray.

The statue was discovered in 1863 by French archaeologist Charles Champoiseau on the nearly inaccessible island of Samothraki in the northern Aegean Sea. When his crew unearthed her, Nike's arms and head were missing. We don't know what the face of victory looked like. Yet art historians don't mourn over the lost head; rather, they claim the finest part of her has been preserved. Her torso—her core—prevailed. Her midriff shows such artistry, such motion, such balance between delicacy and force. Many scholars speculated that she held a long trumpet in her outstretched arms, which was a common image imprinted on coins. Then, in 1950, a ten-inch marble hand was excavated, a hand that matched the proportions and Parian marble of Nike. The open hand suggests a gesture, perhaps an offering or a call. I imagined the palm faced up, holding a token of some kind.

In the Greek language, Νίκη is the feminine form of Νίκο, or Nick, the word for victory. In the Greek Orthodox Church, Saint Nikolaos is the patron saint of sailors. The protector of those at sea. On the *SV Interlude*, had I received Saint Nikolaos's protection? Or Nike's? Or both?

When I interviewed my mother in 2012, she told me that after I'd left for Oceans Abroad, she kept finding coins. "I went to the pool three times a week," she said, "and I found coins every time I walked through the parking lot. Quarters even. Right by my car."

Since I can remember, my mother has suffered from recurrent kidney stones. Swimming helps take her mind off the pain, and it keeps her in phenomenal shape. She invited me to a water aerobics class over winter break once. Steam rose from the warm water and frosted the women's gray hair. The knee lifts we did caused the water to be uneven, which made me nauseous. I had to sit at the edge of the pool, watching elderly women do what I could not.

"I was showered with coins," Mom said. "I put them in my car, in the cup holder. I was afraid to spend them—I didn't know what would happen. I was finding coins so often I thought, *This has to be a sign. Someone's trying to reach me but can't.* And I thought, *Oh my gosh, maybe it's you.*

"Then Marika and I went to see that movie, *Master and Commander.* The whole film is on a ship with rough waters. I just lost it. I broke down four times at the movie theater. Sobbing, trying to hide it. I was so emotional. All I could think of was you reaching out for help. It was shortly thereafter, within days, that I got the call. You were coming home."

As she told me about the coins, I kept seeing Nike in my imagination, holding out her palm to my mother, that smooth palm, open with a coin. *Take this. Your daughter needs you.*

"They say a parent gets a sixth sense," my mother said. "You just feel for your children. You're in tune with them. When you see their pain, you feel their pain." She sighed. "The mysteries of life."

At college one night in late November, I awoke to the sound of crying. Feeling my damp cheeks, I realized the sobs had come from me. I had my own dorm room now, the same high-ceilinged room Jae and Samantha had lived in the year before. The night was still. A shaft of moonlight was projected on the floor. I stared at the rectangle of light, trying to remember what I'd been dreaming about. A silver treasure chest. My cheek sank back into the damp pillow and I relived not the dream, but the memory.

At the airport in Helena, right before I boarded the plane for Oceans Abroad, Marika told me to check my duffle bag for a surprise she and Mom packed for me. After I fell sick on the ship, I remember finding the package under my snorkel goggles. The wrapping paper was purple with shiny swirls. I set the box on my blanket. It looked foreign in the stark bunk room, as if I hadn't seen colors in days. Maybe I hadn't.

I unwrapped the package on my bunk bed, retracing the folds my mother or sister had made. Inside was a little wooden treasure chest painted silver. My fingers shook as I unlatched the clasp. A rainbow of confetti filled the inside: stars, moons, squares. Buried within the confetti were small strips of paper. I unfolded one and saw the curved handwriting of my sister. I unfolded another: my mother's script saying how proud of me she was for pursuing my dreams. I realized then that she and Marika had tracked down the people most significant in my life and tucked their words into this treasure chest. I opened one more, a piece of paper from Nick. In his slanted penmanship, he had written: *Don't look behind. I'm at your back.*

In the dorm room, my cheek sank deeper into the pillow. I hadn't thought about that treasure chest in nearly four years. I didn't even know where to find it. But I had remembered Nick's words. I decided right then, with the moon shining on the floor, that I wanted Nike of Samothraki tattooed between my shoulder blades.

Around the same time, Nick wanted to get the J. R. R. Tolkien quote *Not all those who wander are lost* translated into Greek and tattooed on his body. In the end, he designed a tattoo with a Greek key instead, which expressed the same message. The Greek key, or meander pattern, as it's called by art historians, is the path of the quintessential wanderer. It follows not a straight line, but a winding, indirect path. Through bends and twists, the pattern progresses, linking to more bends and twists. The Greek key filled Geometric Period vases nearly three thousand years ago and continues to influence architecture around the world. The meander pattern has endured. Nike of Samothraki has endured. Nick and I—we have endured.

The following semester, I enrolled in a creative nonfiction course. I had taken a fiction class freshman year in Oregon and a poetry class in California, so I thought I was prepared to take an upper level creative writing course. But fiction was different. In a short story, I could write something that wasn't directly about me. I could speak through my characters, fulfill my aspirations, or rewrite my history. In my poems, I had alluded to my illnesses but had never used the "I" pronoun.

Nonfiction was not as ambiguous. There was no *based on a true story* disclaimer. No proxy. The subject was I, me, myself expressing my own dreams and disappointments. But I didn't know this when I enrolled. I really didn't know anything about nonfiction, except that it was related to nature writing...maybe?

On the first day of class, I walked through the damp quad to Beckham Hall. After climbing three flights up the banistered staircase, I entered a room that contained a large table surrounded by squashy chairs. This, I came to learn, was a typical workshop-styled classroom. Our instructor, Professor Theodore, had an unerring passion for "The Craft" of writing. He also had the ability, I half-believed, to see right through that expressionless marble face I wore.

When I imagined the class reading about my life, an increasing sense of vulnerability tormented me. I tried to negate this feeling by applying foundation, blush, eye shadow, shirts, scarves, jackets. Class was in the afternoon, so I had all morning to don my armor. That's what I was doing: applying layers to create a wall between myself and my self. But the more foundation I applied, the more I saw the acne pocks at my temples and the oversized pores around my nostrils. The more clothes I wore, the more defenseless I felt.

Every Thursday, two students' pieces were workshopped in class. The writers had to sit quietly and listen while the rest of the class critiqued their essays. I was less concerned with having my writing picked apart than with the fact that my peers and professor would be scrutinizing my personal history. When reflecting on my life, all mirrors eventually reflected white pills and wet decks. How long could I avoid facing my past? How long could I avoid writing about the ship? Most of my college friends didn't know about the *SV Interlude* or about Lariam. The people who did—Samantha, Jae, Ruby—didn't know I had chronic PTSD that flared up depending on the environment or time of year. How would they judge me? If they found out I had a mental disorder, would I ever look the same to them again?

The first assignment was to write a one-page self portrait, a description of how we saw ourselves. The piece could be in any form, so I wrote a poem. I was studying for the GRE at the time, so I weaved in words like *reticent, resplendent, diaphanous, capricious!*

It was bad. Like pretentious poetry bad.

Our second assignment was a significant moment essay. I'd been reading a lot of Faulkner, so I wrote these long Benjy-like sections: confusing passages emphasizing smells and sounds and incomplete thoughts. Ancient Greek concepts I'd learned in my art history class also appeared in the draft: ethos, stoicism, Platonism, a divine image over reality.

Professor Theodore arranged one-on-one conferences for this second assignment. Reluctantly, I took the stairs to his third-floor office. "Hi, Deme," he said. "Have a seat."

The March sun shone on his bookcase of short story anthologies and essay collections. A French documentary titled *The Gleaners and I* rested on his desk. "You're developing scene well," he said, referring to my draft. "But right when you get to the heart of the piece, you begin deflecting."

I mouthed the word *de-*flect-*ing*. My hands fidgeted with the folder on my lap. "I don't understand."

He set the draft on his desk. "Your use of ancient philosophy is preventing *you* from speaking." I bent over my work. Sure enough, instead of describing my emotions, I had switched into a discussion about Sokrates and his views on love. In another spot, instead of reflecting on the feeling of disappointment, I had discussed Plato's high forms of Truth and Beauty and how they don't exist in true form on earth. I examined the draft a moment longer, trying to hear what it would sound like without the deflections.

It sounded exposed.

"This is right where you need to be," my professor said. "At the heart of it all."

After that office visit, I walked back to my dorm and studied the prompt for our first assignment, the self portrait: *Capture a defining attribute, event, or belief that represents you.* I discarded the crappy poem and started from scratch. On a new document, I typed:

Troy

I watched that film seven times over winter break. In four days. Once by myself, once until I stoically drove my convulsing mother to the emergency room, and more still in between reminding her to take it easy and stay off her feet. I even went to the library, found the ancient tragedies section, and compared different translations. I found the version that sounded closest to the source. I read a 'book' every night before bed, prayed to Athena, memorized epic war speeches.

Though the film strayed from the original text, its art historical accuracy impressed me. Minoan-influenced columns. Elongated proportions. Apotropaic devices. Octopuses or snakes painted onto shields, paradoxically symbolizing death and regeneration. Intricately woven clothing. Textile was perhaps the Greeks' most accomplished artistic skill, the one form that in no way has survived the decay of time. We know this only by delineations on vases, accounts from Homer, Euripides.

What else kept me returning to that film? Was it the mortality angle

Axilles pulled on Briseis? 'The gods envy us,' he told her. 'Life is more beautiful because we are doomed.' Or was it his peering out over the edge of a long-beaked ship, something I barely got to do? His unashamed grief for Patroklos? such Rage? Maybe it was simply the sound of that word: Myrmidons.

After the seventh time, it clicked. I glanced over at my mother: jaw set, kidney stones wracking her elegant body, face hard as marble. I turned back to the screen and beheld Axilles: crumpled in torchlight, hair scattered like rays of sun, pierced ankle darkening the grass. My tears merged with his, accepting our place in the mortal world, finally seeing the trap in fighting to appear invulnerable.

The ship eventually edged into my writing, as it had in my revised self portrait. During workshop one day, a student drew attention to it. "This ship," she said. "You've mentioned it twice now in your writing. What about this ship? Tell us more."

I stared straight ahead at a piece of chalk, debating whether to chuck it, hard, at her forehead or to scribble wildly on the board: *"This ship" is the reason why I'm here writing about my life instead of living it!*

Professor Theodore must've detected my face spasm, because he redirected the conversation. "Let's look at her dialogue," he said, referring to page four. The students turned the page, leaving the ship image behind. I knew then that I couldn't avoid the *SV Interlude* much longer.

"Our next piece," Professor Theodore said in early April, "is the place essay. Choose a significant place, somewhere that means a lot to you, and write about your relationship to it."

Most students wrote about childhood homes, vacation spots, or first cars. I chose to write about the stage and PTSD. These were two significant places where I'd spent considerable time, two places inextricably intertwined. The only way I could write about this subject matter was by pairing it with something enduring, something regenerative. So I structured my piece around the mythical phoenix, a creature with fire-tipped feathers. From ancient Greek, I surmised that the name itself was a paradox: *phoe-*, like Foibos Apollo, the god of light; and *-nix*, Nyx, the dark deity of the night. Day and night, light and dark, health and illness. I thought I might be "deflecting" by incorporating this ancient Greek imagery, so I tried envisioning the structure of the piece without using the phoenix metaphor. But without it, there would be no beauty in the retelling of the past. Only ashes. So I kept following the cycle of the phoenix. When I veiled an emotion with a Platonic ideal, I gave the pen to my heart and promised not to judge what it had to write.

This assignment was the first time I wrote about my mental disorder—the first time I typed P T S D. The proximity of those letters to the first-person "I" on the page made me feel chillingly exposed, yet, somehow, warmly empowered. Releasing my experiences gave me relief. I was finding words for feelings I had masked for so many years. But I was afraid of what remembering might do.

After I typed the first scene I had ever written about the ship, I sat alert in my dorm room, waiting for an upsurge of flashbacks, ready to combat them with Nike and Hawaiian music. But they never came. Just tears. Tears that wet the crook of my neck. Tears that fell between the letters on the keyboard.

I decided to call Irene. I sat at my desk, elbows propped on a spiral notebook, pen ready to write whatever guidance she had to offer. "One major effect of trauma is unshed tears," Irene told me. "Finally crying out the shock. The more tears, the better." I remembered how I had cried that spring I rehearsed the Ifigeneia monologue. Those tears, like these, were the tears of trauma, of loss.

Sometimes while typing at my computer, I analyzed what I was grieving over. The lost dream of sailing? The lead-up and the letdown? Why couldn't I just get over it? Move on? Be happy I was alive? I hadn't lost a family member or friend. But in a way, I had. I lost a version of myself I was never reunited with again. I lost the optimism and fearlessness of youth. I lost a healthy digestive system. But was that enough to grieve over?

156

Losses that don't fit the social norm are what psychologists call ambiguous. Kathleen Gilbert, PhD, writes widely on the topics of loss and grief. She describes how ambiguous losses "lack clarity." The individual struggles to pinpoint "exactly who or what has been lost." Losing a pet, losing someone to AIDS, or having an abortion are examples of ambiguous loss. Because these losses do not fit social norms, society denies mourners permission to mourn. A moral judgment is imposed on the loss and stifles the individual's instinct to grieve, and therefore, to heal.

Losses unrelated to death can also be ambiguous. One example that resonates with me is the loss felt from what Gilbert calls "invisible but disabling" conditions or illnesses. My journey from February 17, 2004, onward has been a battle with factors invisible to the outside world. Irritable bowel syndrome doesn't show up in lab work, scar tissue isn't always detected by imaging devices, and posttraumatic stress disorder has no defining physical attribute.

But what about ambiguous trauma? Experiences not recognized by society? Michelle Flaum Hall, EdD, and Scott Hall, PhD, confirmed my thoughts: "Just as some grief can be disenfranchised, so too can trauma be invalidated or remain unacknowledged." I've spent far too long trying to pinpoint exactly how to explain my experience to others. But I shouldn't need to explain. Or justify. That's not my role.

In Greek, trauma is related to the verb τιτρώσκω (titrosko), "to injure." A more accurate translation is "to pierce." In the *DSM-5*, the following synonyms are used to describe events that can lead to PTSD: traumatic, stressful, catastrophic, aversive, and life-threatening. Often, we think of military combat, sexual assault, natural disaster, or violent acts as traumatic. I've compared my own experience to that list for too many years now: *But I'm not a combat vet. I'm not a survivor of war. I didn't survive a massive earthquake. I don't deserve the PTSD diagnosis.* Yet just because my experience—and countless others that individuals endure—isn't included in a socially recognized list doesn't mean that what we've endured wasn't traumatic, wasn't aversive, wasn't life-threatening. I've kept my experience silent out of fear of being misunderstood or not understood. As the *DSM-5*'s "negative alterations in cognitions and mood" PTSD symptom cluster indicates, we survivors minimize our experiences enough. We don't need others to pierce the wound too.

From this socially unrecognized experience, I earned a perfect score on the posttraumatic stress disorder checklist in both the *DSM-4* and *DSM-5* versions. How's that for being a straight-A student? How's that for putting a numeric value on "invisible but disabling" symptoms? Zooming out from the internal doubts of the individual, according to the National Center for PTSD, "about 8 million adults have PTSD during a given year." The health of our nation depends on our ability to acknowledge the scope of trauma. To consider how many people, symptoms, and events are disenfranchised because of ambiguity.

When I stopped trying to intellectualize my grief and trauma— when I muted my probing, critical mind—I was able to allow myself to grieve, and therefore, to heal. While writing in my dorm room, if I felt intense sadness, I sat back and cried. Allowing the tears to fall was less painful than trying to fight them. After my sadness had been released, I continued writing. If I felt intense anger, I journaled in a notebook until I could write coherently enough to continue the place essay.

Eventually, I reached the transformation section, when from its own ashes the phoenix rises again. I worked late at night. Midnight was usually when I hit my stride. Tuesday nights, Friday nights, it didn't matter. Out with my friends, I'd become inspired and dash back to my dorm room to flesh out a scene. At three in the morning, I'd leap out of bed and write a sentence I finally figured out how to construct. When called upon by the Muses, I wrote. I began to feel it again, that creative energy coursing through my body, shooting from my fingertips, fortifying my arms and calves. It felt like hula, like belting a high C, like being onstage. At last, I was completing the circle, bending around the curve, turning upward.

I never workshopped the place essay in class, never showed it to my peers or my family. The only one who read it was Professor Theodore, before our final portfolios were due.

"Deme, there's such clarity here." We were sitting in his office, the fresh smell of rain wafting through the window. "You are at the heart of this piece."

Hearing those words, my eyes began to well. At first, I tried hiding these quiet tears. I turned my face away and wiped my cheeks with my sleeve. But then I remembered Irene's words and just let them seep. My professor didn't comment on the tears. He didn't treat me differently now that he knew I wrestled with mental health. He simply critiqued my writing.

I thanked him, water still streaming, and slowly descended the three flights of stairs through Beckham Hall. It didn't matter that a few students noticed my tears—because I had found my voice. For the first time since February 17, 2004, I had given words to my injury, my pain, and my grief.

Without intending to, I had uncovered the face of victory.

Grace told me once that she didn't know what to do with her story about Lariam and being misdiagnosed with bipolar disorder. A therapist told her that she didn't have to tell anybody anything. "Only if you want to. Only if you think it will bring you closer to someone."

One night, Grace went to a sports bar in Missoula, where she met a man originally from Great Falls. That night, she told him her entire story. When Grace relayed her night to me, she said, "Half of me thought, *Man, this guy's gonna run*. The other half of me thought, *Well, this is me. He might as well know*." That "guy" would become her future husband.

In college, my story about Lariam and the ship was like a wall separating me from the dating world. What if a boyfriend and I went to a movie that had footage of boats or waves? What if we went to dinner and I had a GI reaction to something I ate? What if he noticed me taking a pill every night? I couldn't let anyone see how I slept: hot pink ear plugs, a sleeping mask, and medication. I chose healing over romance every time. That was more important to my well-being back then.

Eventually, romance became part of the healing process. Almost two years after graduating from college, I finally shared my story with a boyfriend. Luke and I had only been dating for a few months. One night, I told him, "I want to read something to you." I turned on my laptop and opened the place essay from Professor Theodore's creative nonfiction class. Through writing was the only way I could communicate my story.

I read the essay to Luke, slowly but steadily. After the last paragraph, he took my hands in his. "I think people use this phrase too lightly," he said, "but I want you to know that I mean every word. You are a remarkable woman. I love you."

As our relationship grew, I remember coming to the realization that a home isn't just a place. Home is a person, a feeling of safety, a sense of acceptance. Luke was the only person I spoke freely to about my experience on the ship. I'd read him passages from my graduate thesis or share new research I'd found about PTSD. Then we'd talk about our grocery list, or about the heating bill, or about our puppy's obsession with squirrels. What had been off limits for so long was now being integrated into everyday conversations. Talking regularly about Oceans Abroad was desensitizing the trauma. The pain was fading, the fear dissolving. A home was beginning to appear.

Before I met Luke, I had only shared the abridged version of my life. The version without vulnerability. Grace taught me that when you're ready, when you feel safe, and when you truly want to, you can show people who you are. Using the medium of your choice—song, dance, talking, drawing, writing—you can express what makes you remarkable.

ΔI

What suffering must you endure?
~Euripides, *Hekebe*

Why do certain people develop posttraumatic stress disorder while others do not? This question has plagued me for years. One theory is that individuals who have previously experienced a traumatic life event are more likely to develop PTSD after a second traumatic experience. My therapist, Irene, stressed this theory with me. In our early sessions, she pointed to the first traumatic event in my life: divorce.

At the time, her focus on my parents' divorce annoyed me. *I don't want this session spent on them,* I thought. Calling divorce "trauma" sounded a little extreme. *Lots of kids have divorced parents,* I reasoned. *You expect me to believe we've all been traumatized?*

Seven years into my therapy, when I was twenty-seven, Irene instructed me to draw a diagram mapping the two traumas in my life. On a blank page, she told me to draw a small circle and write *I was born* and the words *innocence* and *pure trust.* Around that circle, I drew another one with the words *divorce* and *shock.*

Around the two circles, Irene had me draw a square: *guarded, shielded.* Around the square, another circle: *ship, shock.*

Around all, a square: *GUARD*.

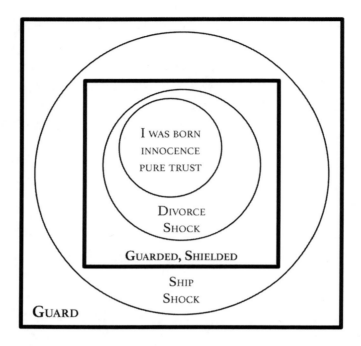

On the paper, I didn't see just circles and squares, nor did I only see a high school senior bearing a colossal shield between herself and the world. I saw, beyond that shield, a little girl with tanned skin and messy curls squatting down to pick up a piece of armor too big for her, trying to make sense of a world that only yesterday had been predictable and warm. In the immediacy of Oceans Abroad, I had overlooked the first time the ground beneath my feet had shaken.

The diagram brought to mind a memory I hadn't been able to figure out until Irene's lesson. A few Decembers after graduating from college, my siblings and I were at Mom's house for Christmas Eve dinner. Christmas Eve at Mom's, Christmas day at Dad's. We kept the tradition into adulthood. A cassette tape of the Manheim Steamrollers played on repeat while we opened presents and ate dinner. "Mom," Nick said at the kitchen table, "do you have any other music? We've been listening to this since we got here."

We laughed. Mom always played Manheim Steamrollers.

"It's Christmas," she replied simply.

Marika got up from the table and shuffled through a basket of old cassettes. She found one dated December 1985, three years before Johnny was born and eight years before our parents divorced. We listened to the tape while passing a tray of Christmas cookies and Greek pastries. We heard me cooing and gurgling, Mom humming to me, Nick interrupting her, Marika conducting the recording, and Dad playfully telling Nick, "Come here, you knucklehead!"

Around the table, Mom, Marika, and Nick were laughing. Johnny had a pleasant but left out kind of smile on his face. They picked the cloves from their honey-soaked baklava and continued eating.

"Demetra!" Marika said.

Everyone turned to look at me.

My face was dripping with tears. "I can't help it," I gulped, trying to control my sobs.

"It's happy," my sister said.

"I know," I cried. Wiping my wet cheeks with sticky hands, I looked at each pair of dry eyes. How did listening to this tape not make my siblings sad? Couldn't they hear the unity of our childhood home? The tears continued pouring. Hearing my parents' young voices must've risen up the trauma that divorce does, in fact, cause.

My siblings and I have been affected by divorce, each in our own ways. The earthquake struck at different times in our personal journeys. Marika and Nick were in middle school, I was in second grade, and Johnny was in daycare. I don't know how my siblings guarded themselves after the divorce or what their shields look like.

Or my parents' shields. What childhood traumas have they endured? What traumas have they absorbed from their parents, who emigrated from their homeland during war? Shock waves reverberating from generation to generation: from the Nazi occupation? the Balkan Wars? the Ottoman rule? the destruction of the Byzantine Empire?

We might never know.

Each of us—we all don armor. We all have experiences that blindside us, experiences we can't order into a linear narrative, ones singed into memory. What pressure we put on ourselves to appear whole; what strength we muster to bear our shields. I am finally able to gaze beyond my second shield to see the first. I am finally able to comprehend, fleetingly, the depths of our collective armor.

After living in California, I began teaching at performing arts camps. I did not feel at ease in my hometown, so I found a different community in which to belong: Venture Theatre in Billings, Montana. Billings is about four hours from Helena, in the eastern part of the state. It is the largest city in Montana, with just over 100,000 people. Most of the city lies in a valley beneath long sandstone cliffs. Venture Theatre was located in the historic downtown, across from an old train depot. The theatre had been converted from a warehouse. The main auditorium had sloped seating and a concrete floor marked with old yellow parking lot lines. The building housed several classrooms and dance studios, which made it an ideal teaching facility. Venture was a sister theatre to Grandstreet and modeled its summer program after theirs. The summer camp ran from 9:00 a.m. to 5:00 p.m. on weekdays for two weeks at a time. Each morning, announcements were held in the auditorium, then students broke into classes for acting, movement, and voice lessons. The entire camp ate lunch at a park downtown by the courthouse. In the afternoon, students rehearsed for their culminating showcase performance.

Venture Theatre, and as an extension, Billings, became my new home in Montana. It's where I went not to worship theatre anymore, but to honor my body. I danced, choreographed, and taught hula. I was in the presence of other college and post-college instructors making a living off of their passions. What's more, I was me. The people I was surrounded by—the instructors, the camp kids, their parents—knew nothing of my obscure past, that I'd been trapped, ill and uncared for, on a ship. I forgot about it myself. I was living in the present, fulfilling my artistic goals, doing what I loved in a community that saw me for me, that saw me as I saw myself: a woman with a passion for performing.

At Venture, I found myself in a role I had not expected. Instead of teaching acting, I was assigned to the dance classes. For five summers, I taught movement to theatre's youth. My years of musical theatre and Irish dance, my stints with ballet and modern, my cheerleading seasons, and my newfound alignment with hula were all culminating into this new role. Not being classically trained and having never mastered one single dance form, I didn't consider myself a "real" dancer. But in front of the children's wide eyes and eager faces, I began to realize that to them, I was.

One morning, I led my class of seventh graders through warm-ups. As we leaned into a hurdle stretch, I quizzed them: "Why should you breathe?"

"So you don't forget your lines."

"So you don't forget your choreography."

"So you don't get nervous."

"Yes," I smiled, switching legs. "We breathe to alleviate stress. We breathe to stay relaxed, in the present moment. As performers, we cannot miss a beat."

The tranquil voice of Israel Kamakawiwoʻole drifted from the boom box. I had made a CD of calming songs, mostly Hawaiian, to play while we stretched.

During warm-ups, the students practiced breathing from their diaphragm. Lying with their back on the ground, they placed a hand on their stomach. "As you inhale," I said, "feel your tummy rise to the ceiling. As you exhale, feel it sink into the floor." Glimpsing at the reflection in the dance studio mirrors, I saw twelve hands gently rise and fall. I lay on the floor too and joined in the emptying and filling of lungs. I was not a teacher who told kids what to do; I breathed with them, stretched with them, and danced with them.

In the morning, I taught three movement classes: one to high schoolers, one to middle schoolers, and one to elementary students. The first few summers I taught, the elementary classes were the most challenging. The kids never held still. They didn't seem to appreciate the calming Hawaiian music. They giggled at the sounds the singers made and asked if we could listen to Katy Perry or Sean Kingston.

"Absolutely not," I'd reply. "'Fire Burning' will not relax your body."

Eventually, I learned to loosen up and work with their rambunctious energy rather than against it. Warm-ups with the younger groups were not as tranquil, but they were entertaining. Our calf muscles became "baby cows," triceps "triceratops," and hamstrings "Hamlets."

At the end of each two-week session, a showcase was presented to parents and family members. Each showcase had about ten students in it, grades three through twelve. Directing showcases allowed instructors to integrate their directorial, scriptwriting, and classroom management skills. Each showcase ran about ten minutes long, each with its own flair. Some were written completely by students—usually the ones about Harry Potter or vampires—others by instructors. I always added dance into mine, choreographing numbers and selecting songs that could be integrated into a storyline.

One summer, I created a showcase based on Ed Sullivan's variety show, sprinkled with celebrities like Elvis and the Beatles. We rehearsed in the same dance studio where I taught my morning classes. By showcase rehearsal time—3:30 to 5:00—the kids were hungry, hyper, and sweaty. Most of my cast chose their own roles, but a fourth-grade girl named Felicity offered no suggestions. She had thick black hair and the ability to stay on beat and hit exact dance moves.

"How about Cher?" I asked her.

"Who's that?" she spat.

I turned to my high school assistant, Lena. "Are we that old?"

Lena had been my assistant for two years in a row. She wore a stack of friendship bracelets she and other assistants braided in the greenroom. "You know," she explained to Felicity, "Sonny and Cher. Super powerful voice. Cher."

Felicity looked at us like we were speaking French.

"Your parents probably know her," I said. "When you go home tonight, can you look her up on the computer?"

"I *guess.*"

At the daily staff meetings, Felicity was receiving mixed reviews from the instructors and assistants. Some commented that she was very timid in class, while others contradicted with "I can't get her to shut up!"

"Really?" the camp director asked. "That sweet thing? How is she in rehearsals?"

"Well, she's a little..." I looked to Lena across the table.

"She's either bouncing off the walls or too shy to do anything!" Lena finished.

"Yes," we all concurred.

During showcase rehearsal, I gave Felicity the same note every afternoon: "Speak up! We can't hear you in this dance studio, which isn't that big. Once we start practicing on the main stage, no one will be able to hear you." Lena took her into the hallway. With Felicity at one end and Lena at the other, they worked on sending Felicity's voice all the way down the hall.

As Cher, Felicity was the leader in the showcase's final dance number. Positioned in a V formation, she was the focal point of the V, the closest to the audience, with no one in her periphery. When we rehearsed the dance on the main stage, she looked over her shoulder to watch the other students.

"Felicity! Eyes forward!"

Before long, camp was almost over. Lena and I held a private meeting at lunchtime. "She knows the dance," Lena said.

"I know. She never misses a beat when we rehearse offstage. She has potential. I saw it that first day of rehearsals. It's too late—I can't recast her role. What is it? A lack of confidence? Should I re-block the song? Break the V formation and just do rows?"

"No," Lena said. "She's got it. She just needs to get used to being up front."

"And still, I can hardly hear her lines," I said.

"I'm working on it."

On the day of the camp's showcase performances, I met my cast in the dance studio. "Look how handsome and beautiful you all are!"

The boy playing Sonny was wearing bell bottoms, the fifth grader who played Elvis was swiveling his hips, and "The Beatles" were practicing their British accents in front of the mirrors.

"Where's Felicity?"

The kids shrugged.

Panicked, I turned to Lena.

She rushed out of the room to call Felicity's house.

I turned on Hawaiian music, hoping to calm my own nerves. My little celebrities and I formed a circle and began stretching. "We've got to be warmed up for our big performance." I smiled, trying to hide my panic.

"Where's Felicity?" the third grader who played Shirley Temple asked.

"She'll be here," I said. "Take off your tap shoes, Julie, and just focus on stretching."

Lena arrived a few minutes later. "Look who I found!" Behind her was Felicity and a woman she clearly resembled.

I got up from the circle and walked over to them. Felicity sported a fur vest and suede boots. "Oh my gosh, she looks just like a '70s version of Cher."

Her mother smiled and introduced herself.

"Go join the cast," I said to Felicity.

She skipped away, her sleek hair bouncing left to right.

I was about to make up a compliment about how fantastic Felicity was, but her mother spoke before me. "I wanted to thank you," she said. "This play is all she talks about at home. She shows me her dance every night."

"She's very talented," I said, hoping she wouldn't mess up in front of the audience.

Her mother looked at Felicity and the other kids warming up on the floor. "This camp has been so good for her," she said. "It's really brought her out of her shell."

Lena and I exchanged looks.

"Since the divorce, she hasn't been herself."

My jaw dropped.

Felicity's mother looked young, not more than thirty. Yet her skin was strained, pulled tight at the temples. "It's so nice to hear her giggling," she said. Her eyes began to water. She wiped a tear before her eyeliner could smudge.

I realized then how much I'd expected of Felicity. No instructor or assistant had checked in with her. No one had taken her aside to ask her how she was doing. I felt terrible.

When it was our turn to perform, Lena ushered the cast backstage, where they took their places behind the curtain. I sneaked up to the sound booth to run the music. From the back of the house, I watched the kids entertain a packed audience of their parents, relatives, and friends. I heard every line they spoke, even Felicity's. They danced the choreography, with Felicity as their leader. Her movements were sharp, determined. Divorce may have shaken her world, but during the showcase performance, she knew the ground upon which she danced.

I've thought a lot about Felicity since reconsidering the impact divorce has on children. Maybe theatre camp had been a place where she was reminded not of a divided house, but instead to breathe, to speak clearly, to count to eight while dancing.

Like Felicity, I began theatre when I was nine, after my parents divorced. At theatre school, I wasn't reminded of the ever-widening split at home. I wasn't practicing what I'd say to *this* family friend versus *that* family friend depending on his or her allegiance to either parent and how what I said might circulate around our small town. I was practicing my lines, diaphragm support, three-point turns and alto harmony. Onstage, I could predict the outcome of my actions because they had been rehearsed. Though I didn't know how to make my parents happy, I did know how to bring them back together as my audience in the house at Grandstreet Theatre.

Another prominent theory explaining why certain people develop PTSD has less to do with the event itself, and more to do with their return to everyday life. Even after traumatic events that don't take place abroad or away from home, such as domestic violence or molestation, there is an attempted return to what was once familiar. The manner in which people are received by their peers and communities post-event plays a crucial role in their recovery from trauma.

Take World War II veterans, for example. When soldiers returned home, generally speaking, they were welcomed back as heroes. Parades were held in their honor, and trees were draped with yellow ribbons. They had fought "The Good War." But when soldiers returned from Vietnam, there were few open arms and fewer celebrations. They had fought in a war that divided a nation. They had fought amid home front protests. They did not experience a welcome homecoming. With the recent return of soldiers from Iraq, Afghanistan, and other war-torn regions, it is imperative that they feel they are being welcomed home. Their recovery may hinge upon it.

In a study examining former Nepalese child soldiers, medical anthropologist Brandon Kohrt, MD and PhD, observed the influence returning to one's former environment has on trauma recovery. In the *New York Times* article "A New Focus on the 'Post' in Post-Traumatic Stress," author David Dobbs writes about Dr. Kohrt's research: "All 141 in the study, 5 to 14 years old when they joined the rebels, experienced violence and other events considered traumatic, aside from their separation from family. Yet their postwar mental health depended not on their exposure to war but on how their families and villages received them." Dr. Kohrt found that children whose villages welcomed them home with rituals or acts of reintegration suffered minimal effects of trauma. The same did not hold true for those who received little support from their communities upon returning home. Dobbs writes, "In villages where the children were stigmatized or ostracized, they suffered high, persistent levels of post-traumatic stress disorder." Based on my own experience, I too believe the homecoming is equally—if not more—influential than a history of past trauma.

When I returned, I was not reintegrated into my high school community. The administration's reluctance to reinstate my valedictorian status, not to mention its debate about whether or not I could even graduate, negatively impacted the condition of my return. To an honor student, your work is your identity, and if your hard work is not being acknowledged, then neither are you.

Very little is needed to make someone feel welcomed: *Glad to see you. Glad you're back.* A hug. That's all it takes. After recuperating at home, I drove myself to high school. With no explanation, I reappeared in class, like a familiar stranger. Mrs. Presley was the only teacher I remember who welcomed me back. She taught a fiction elective my senior year. I had taken her class fall semester, and when I returned, it was the only elective other than choir that I continued taking.

"Joining us from last semester is Jamie," she told the students.

I was sitting in a row near her desk, looking down at my oversized water bottle.

"We're very glad to have her here, with us."

In her welcoming, I heard an acknowledgement of the seriousness of my health condition. She was thankful not just that I had returned to class, but that I had come back at all.

The students in that class never asked me about the ship. I never felt like I had to justify or explain myself. I was able to move forward, if only in that room, because my peers had accepted my return.

While primary communities for teenagers include school and home, secondary communities include extracurricular activities like jobs, sports teams, and clubs. When I returned to high school, the student council kind of invited me back, and kind of didn't. I remember my vice president saying I should come to meetings, but I was never given information about where or when they were held. What was I supposed to do? Stalk the halls at lunchtime, peeking into classrooms to see where they were? Because I was not re-welcomed into this former community, I felt excluded. I believed the group that had once respected me didn't want me anymore. Maybe I looked as though I had moved past high school clubs.

But I hadn't.

As trivial as I think this sounds, not going back to some stupid high school student council still rips me up inside. Believe me, I wish it didn't. But here they are: the tears I never cried spring semester of my senior year because I was too shell-shocked to process emotion then.

I understand now that what I needed was to participate in the same activities I had before the event. Instead, I became separated from my classmates. It's hard to identify what came first, the isolation or the shame. Because I was isolated from former communities, I felt ashamed. Because I felt ashamed, I further isolated myself from what was once familiar and supportive.

In retrospect, it's easier to identify communities that could've helped me reintegrate back into high school. I think the community that had the most potential to offer support was my choir, a group of sixteen young women, many of whom performed at Grandstreet Theatre too. We were a tight-knit group, and eventually we created what we called "Circle Time." Sitting on the tile floor of the choir room, we confided in each other about crushes, breakups, and other stresses in our teenage lives. Circle Time was a nonjudgmental, confidential space where we could share whatever we felt. Even our conductor, Mr. Williams, valued Circle Time. He saw it as a bonding activity that strengthened his singers' ability to harmonize and blend as a cohesive ensemble. If we rehearsed well, he often gave us the last ten minutes of class to have Circle Time while he went into his office to prepare for his other choirs, always shutting the door to give us privacy. The girls had been with me through the application process for Oceans Abroad, and they'd thrown a farewell party for me before I left for the Philippines.

The day I returned to choir, I pulled up a chair at my old spot, next to Samantha in the alto section. As the girls trickled in, they noticed me and rushed over, asking if I was okay. I remember feeling overwhelmed by their bombardment of concern. Luckily, the choir president motioned to form a circle. As we were setting our music folders down and gathering on the floor, Mr. Williams walked out of his office.

"Time to rehearse," he said. "We have a lot to do this week."

I could tell that the girls were torn between obeying their teacher and supporting their friend. "But Jamie just got back!" one of them argued.

"If there's time afterward, you can have Circle Time," Mr. Williams said.

We rehearsed until the bell rang.

The choir was preparing for an upcoming competition. That weekend, the group was traveling to Spokane, a six-hour bus ride away. I felt wary of traveling so soon after Oceans Abroad. My parents, and even Dr. Pitney, advised against going on the trip. I remember feeling relieved I had a doctor's note to explain why I couldn't go.

With our intensive rehearsals that week, we never had a chance for Circle Time. When the girls returned from Spokane, I felt left out by their references and jokes. Any chance of confiding in them had passed.

I see now that going on the choir trip could've offered a chance for me to talk about my experience with my peers. It could've helped me begin to process my emotions and soften my critical mind. I've imagined the dim light of a hotel room with the fifteen girls lounging on beds and hugging pillows as they listened to my story, siding with me when the ship staff insisted I was fine, and consoling me when I shared that I felt like I had let everyone down, including them.

Unfortunately, that never happened.

I wish I could have traded a farewell party for a welcome home party, which is, in itself, an act of reintegration. Before leaving for Oceans Abroad, my friends and family threw me not one, but three farewell parties: the intimate choir party, a huge surprise party attended by high school and Grandstreet friends and alumni, and a family party of my favorite Greek foods. When I returned from Cambodia, blistered and emaciated, no welcome home parties were thrown. Nor was there any event that celebrated my return. Why would there have been? None of us knew how integral the homecoming phase is for trauma survivors. None of us even knew I had endured trauma. After decades, our nation is only beginning to recognize the role the post-event environment plays in saving people from social isolation.

As I continue to visit my hometown, I move in one of three directions.

One: I feel as though it's not my hometown that's unable to see me in the present, but me. When I return, I am the one who thinks of me as a senior in high school. When I return, I pick up where I left off, which was February 17, 2004.

Two: I feel in the present, independent of the event.

Three: I feel in the present, until a reminder yanks me into the past. While in Helena one spring break, I grabbed an old peacoat from Mom's house. I reached into the coat pockets and found an invitation for the huge surprise party my friends had thrown. I thought it was an old receipt until I unfolded the piece of paper. *No need to bring anything, but more food is always a good thing and anything else you'd think Jamie would like.* Sometime after the party, a friend had given the invitation to me. "I passed them out in English class when you weren't looking," I remember her saying with a grin. *Jamie is leaving to spend a semester abroad, so let's make this something she will remember!*

Are reminders of the past holding me back? Should I just throw away every single scrap of paper, every object, every article of clothing linked to the event? Will that erase it from my present? Will that kill the shame that rekindles when I return to my hometown? Segregate, sever, burn, and disintegrate?

I've held onto an old pair of underwear I've had since high school. Its pink-and-white stripes are faded, the two colors nearly indistinguishable. I packed the underwear for the ship. I know this because it used to have a nametag on it. Along with the uniforms I had my mother throw out, Oceans Abroad sent a sheet of personalized nametags to label my belongings. I can't remember if the nametags were self-adhesive or iron-on. Either way, Marika put them on each item in my duffle bag, including every single sock and even the duffle bag itself. When I saw her handiwork, I started laughing. "You *literally* stuck those on everything!"

Sometime after I returned, I peeled off all the nametags I could find. They were cloth-like, so I couldn't tear them like paper. I remember being angry that I couldn't tear them, couldn't shred them into unrecognizable pieces that would disintegrate into the trash.

I've kept the faded underwear for a decade now. I don't wear it; because it's stretched out, it makes my butt look dumpy. It's just folded, in my drawer, between my other underwear. Unlike the surprise invitation that popped into my life, the underwear doesn't jolt me back to the past. It is predictable. Every time I open my top drawer, I expect it to be there. This faded underwear is one of the few objects I have left that was with me on the ship. We went together. I've also kept my neon green goggles and snorkel, a pair of white-and-orange ankle socks, some books, some CDs, Johnny's portable CD player, and, well, I think that's it.

I found out nine years later that although I told my mother to pitch all the Oceans Abroad apparel, she kept four items: the shiny green coat with the Oceans Abroad emblem embroidered onto it, the heavy duty rain jacket and matching overall pants, and the black duffle bag. When Mom showed them to me, she looked cautious, hesitant, like she had no idea how her daughter would react.

I wasn't afraid of seeing them as I had been when I returned. I wasn't angry; I didn't want to torch them. "Thank you," I said, "for keeping these."

She sighed. "I'm so happy you're okay that I kept them. I just thought, maybe, you'd want to have them again someday." Her eyes welled with tears.

These four items still say JAMIE PERROS. These four items, along with the underwear, portable CD player, music, books, socks, and goggles, are proof that I didn't return alone.

EPSILON

Transfiguration:
the resolution, whether
through catastrophe or victory

ΔΙΙ

With words, the mind takes flight.

~Aristofanes, *Birds*

A plush kitty keychain dangled from my tote bag. Her fur was white, her dress pastel pink. On the train, the gentle colors soothed me. The softness grounded me. Propping the bag on my lap, I wriggled the keychain off and cradled the toy in my hand.

Three times a week, I rode the commuter rail from Providence to Boston for my master's program in creative writing. I worked at the university during the day and attended classes at night. By Thursday of each week, I was exhausted and overstimulated. Loud train noises bombarded my senses—people chattering, passengers snoring, metal screeching, lights blaring, heavy doors slamming shut. I put in earbuds to mute the sounds and wore sunglasses to dim the lights. I held the kitty.

But I have no filter. In my head everything collides.

Against my will, I am catapulted back to the *SV Interlude*.

The ship's billowing sails incite adventure. Its mopped deck holds the promise of tales to come. With waves propelling me forward, I sense a grand voyage: like that of *Treasure Island, Pirates of the Caribbean*, Odysseus and his crew, Axilles and his Myrmidons. Accompanied

by fifty other high school seniors from around the world, we board
the tall ship, our vessel to vibrant sites and exotic worlds.

In my bunk, I unpack my duffle bag. I change out of my turtle-
neck and into a lavender tank top. As I adjust the tank top in front of a
bathroom mirror, I notice hives blanketing my chest.

"Heat rash," the ship nurse says.

Lariam's prescription drug information explains that "skin rash"
is among "the most frequently observed adverse experiences."

The first days at sea, nearly everyone is seasick. They feel dizzy,
nauseous, tired. I feel this too. The FDA's medication guide to Lariam
provides a list of "common" side effects: loss of balance, dizziness,
nausea, vomiting, and diarrhea. So, diagnosed with seasickness and
undiagnosed with common side effects of Lariam, I take the white pill
each Wednesday.

While everyone else climbs the masts, ties anchor knots, or
decorates their bunk below deck, I convulse over the toilet. While everyone else memorizes sailing terms, admires the varnished captain's
wheel, or sips minestrone soup in the messroom, I slip into sleep.

One night in my bottom bunk, I dream my dad and I are on the
bed of a semitruck. The truck is wheeling out of control, screeching
its brakes and protecting us from fire and asphalt. Meteors streak
above. We grasp the truck bed, the metal cutting into our palms. A
huge rock ricochets off the semi and hits my father square in the
back. His body rolls off the truck before I can grab his soaked shirt.
Between the tears, I can't make out what is fire and what is blood.

Suddenly, the semi dodges a meteorite, tilting the truck. My
fingers slide—a streak of red—my head skids into the pavement—
bouncing, hard—and I die.

"Bad dreams" are another common side effect of taking Lariam.
Mine are apocalyptic.

It's so simple. The skin allergy so visible. The side effects so copious.
But misdiagnosed, I swallow a white pill each Wednesday.

When we reach Cambodia, representatives from an important
government office will tour the ship to witness firsthand Oceans

Abroad's unique academic and nautical program. In preparation, we clean the vessel while still at sea. My assigned chore is to mop the classroom. The more water I swish between desk chairs and table legs, the more the room permeates with an odor of fish. The more I blot the floor, the more debris smears into the wood. Elbows collapsing at my sides, I sit down to rest.

"What are you doing?" my team's counselor cries, entering the classroom. "You used unchanged water. You didn't even add soap!"

On deck, my team members stop polishing the railing and washing the portal windows. They enter the room with scrunched up noses, waving their hands to dissipate the smell. They narrow in on me sitting at a desk chair.

The counselor yanks the mop handle from my hand. A student dumps the bucket over the railing and returns with clear, sudsy water.

Humiliated, I stumble out.

I pass the messroom, where Team A is scrubbing tables.

I stagger down the stairs, where Team C is wiping.

I try stepping over rags and hands. "Watch it!" a girl named Ashley or Hilary or Lindsay snaps. Team C's counselor follows me, walking down the corridor, his untucked shirt billowing. Slamming my bunk door in his face, I collapse onto my bed.

Hot tears rush down my cheeks.

Each bunk room has its own small bathroom and two sets of stiff bunk beds. Each room is shared by four same-gendered students. I don't know the names of my bunkmates, but one is from Louisiana—Brittany, maybe—one from Spain, and the other I don't know anything about at all.

Maybe there are only three of us.

The two or three of them gently prod me to go to class and politely announce when lunch is being served. One afternoon, "Brittany" pops her head in the room, exclaiming, "Someone just spotted dolphins leaping at the prow of the ship!"

But the trek upstairs is too exhausting. The ship's deck is too slick. Teachers' lectures too droning. Writing assignments too disorienting.

I am a valedictorian candidate at my high school.

Dolphins are my favorite animal.

While my peers adjust to their sea legs, I stop using mine. Eventually, my quads don't pound when I try to stand up. My calves don't spasm between sheets from disuse. I drift from bunk bed to bathroom, faintly feeling my feet on the floor. The drug information explains that "infrequent adverse events" of Lariam include "muscle weakness" and "muscle cramps."

Though I stop eating, I continue vomiting. After hanging over the toilet, I spin around just in time for my anus to spew diarrhea. The stench makes me vomit again. "Abdominal pain" and "loose stools or diarrhea" are among the "most frequently reported adverse events."

These episodes usually occur in the daytime while my bunk-mates are in class. At least, I like to think they aren't just outside the flimsy accordion door.

After what remnants of waste product are expelled, I retch stomach bile. After that, I simply dry heave. No more splashes speckling my glasses. No more chunks catching in my hair. The dry heaves are clean, silent, effortless.

One afternoon, I decide to wash away my sickness. I brush my teeth, trying to scrub the taste of acid off my tongue. I take a shower, which I haven't attempted since boarding the ship.

I turn on the water. Droplets sprinkle onto my hand.

I step into the shower and let water spill over me. I look down at my naked body for the first time since changing into the lavender tank top. My eighteen-year-old breasts look depleted. My ribcage protrudes, my hip bones jut out, my belly swoops inward. I wrap my thin arms around my torso, trying to fill the gaping void. Inspecting my thighs, I see they lack their once-prided muscle. No tight glutes from clipping onstage in character shoes. No indication of robust diaphragm support as I belted a high B in *Honk!* No sign of countless push-ups in my bedroom. No trace of vivacious smile in black-and-white 8x10 headshots.

I do not recognize this body.

Turning off the shower, I grasp for my beach towel and frantically begin drying. But the colors are too vibrant. The patterns too chaotic. The fabric too loud.

The towel drops to the floor. Trapped in the cubicle, my toes grip the moist linoleum. My jaw clenches. A horribly exposed body reflects in the mirror.

The naked body of θάνατος.

Enter psychiatric side effects of Lariam: restlessness, anxiety, paranoia, hallucinations.

I am moved into the top bunk of the nurse's room. Maybe my bunkmates are annoyed. Maybe the staff wants to monitor me, make sure I'm not just acting seasick, just seeking attention, just finding excuses to fail out of classes and skip mandatory deck duty.

The nurse, Ingrid, never consults my medical forms. Never considers that I am taking, like everyone else, some form of an antimalarial.

Nurse Ingrid acts important. I don't know what keeps her running in and out of the room so much. Maybe she distributes bandages, checks sore throats, misdiagnoses more rashes.

The door to the bunk room is made of metal, with the titan ability to seal shut if water were ever to spill below deck. Constantly, the door opens. Constantly, it slams shut. Constantly, it screeches open again.

That door is the gateway to hell.

Each time its handle turns, my heart jolts. Each time it slams shut, knives stab my ears. At night the crewmen—with their blond hair blending into their blond skin—hurl open the door, thrashing the darkness with axes. The ax blades are massive and scorching hot. Singed. Shining.

This happens day and night.

So I try to stay awake. I chew peppermint gum. I listen to musicals on my portable CD player. I read *The Return of the King* with a miniature reading lamp Mrs. Presley gave me as a going away present.

Still, the crewmen thrash.

Deep in the night, I lie awake in the top bunk, vigilant. I scan the dark room. The door handle quivers. Holding my breath, I grope the sheets for my teddy bear, Kirby. He has a faded blue bow and two softened tags. When I was little, I used to rub the silky tags between my fingers as I fell asleep. But Kirby is nowhere to be found. He wasn't with me when I boarded the ship. I forgot to pack him. He's sitting at the foot of my bed in Montana. I think of my bed back home, its antique bedframe, ivy comforter, clouds of pillows. I feel the starched sheets, thin mattress pad, wooden planks.

The door crashes open.

I scream.

A single crewman creeps into the room, eyes glinting like his raised ax blade. Hugging the Tolkien book to my chest, I plead to be transported to the White City where Aragorn reigns.

No blow strikes.

My eyes dart to each corner of the room, searching the darkness for the axman. The desk. The chair. The shelves. Where is he? Has he left? I don't know. I can't tell. I can't decipher reality from nightmare, nightmare from reality.

In the bed below me, Ingrid sleeps. She can sleep through all the invasions in the world because she snores. I hate the sound of her snoring.

I hate the sound of the ship engine even more.

Loud.

Droning.

Lurching.

Screeching.

Loud.

Droning.

Lurching.

Screeching.

Tirelessly. Ominously.

No escape from its noise.

No release from this mental prison.

The kitty keychain grounded me. Her fur soothed me. But as I stepped off the platform and walked through Providence Station's parking lot, the train noises still collided. The lights still glared. So I plunged a hand into my tweed peacoat. The pockets were lined in nylon. They reminded me of my mother's silky cheek. They felt like Kirby's worn tags.

Finally—one hand clutching the plush kitty, the other touching nylon—I was comforted. I began to cry. I didn't cry from a sense of helplessness, nor did I cry out of fear. I cried because I was being comforted, because I was allowing myself to be.

I opened my car door and sat inside without starting the ignition. My mind sifted through its stimuli and resurfaced. I didn't rush it. I gave it time.

I gave myself time.

When I was ready, I started my car and drove the short trip home. I climbed the stairs to our third floor apartment. Luke was already asleep, so I entered the bedroom without turning on the lights. He was on his surgery rotation in medical school and had to wake up at 4:30 a.m. to round on post-op patients. I didn't want to worry him. I didn't want to burden him with my burden.

It was, after all, 2011. I was not a senior in high school anymore. I graduated from college; I was in an MFA program; I was twenty-six years old. Refusing to believe the critical voice in my head—*Get over it! You should be over this by now!*—I quietly pinched open the kennel at the foot of the bed. Our nine-month-old Westie, Lila, bumbled out. I picked her up and pressed her gently to my chest. I took her into the living room, where we sat on the couch, me holding her, she letting me. Her fur was soft, white, like the kitty's. It was silky, warm, like my mother's cheek. Blinking up at me, Lila slowly licked my nose. I heard her gentle breathing and felt my own breaths grow gentle too.

Eventually, I tiptoed back into the bedroom. Lila burrowed into her kennel, and I climbed under the comforter. Luke stirred. Wrapping his arm around me, he asked, "How was your day?"

I didn't answer.

"Sweetie?"

"It was fine," I said, fighting back tears. "I don't think I can do this."

"Do what?"

"Any of it." I covered my head with a pillow.

He uncovered my head and brushed the hair from my face.

"The commute," I whispered. "And writing about the ship. I feel like I'm just waiting. Waiting for the next thing to implode or come crashing down." I thought about Oceans Abroad. I thought about California and theatre and everything I'd sought out to do yet never completed because of mefloquine and PTSD. "I had to redefine myself. Redefine my entire life. And what if grad school doesn't work out either? What if I get sick or can't make the commute?"

Luke clutched my hand. "Don't you ever live like that, waiting for the other shoe to drop. That is imprisonment."

Tears slid down my temples.

"Keep writing," Luke said.

"It's killing me," I said back.

"No, it's liberating you."

He's right. We're both right.

After my episode on the train, I started having phone sessions with Irene again. I'd gone three years without needing therapy, but in graduate school I was writing full-time about my past, and incidents began to occur that interfered with functioning from day to day.

One night, I was reading a classmate's workshop piece on the commute back to Providence. *My father kept his business open, except for a brief interlude*, he'd written. *Interlude*. I hadn't seen that word typed out, it seemed, since reading the brochures years ago. This was before I had named the vessel in my workshop pieces. I was still referring to it as *the ship* or *the program*. I slapped the word on the page, as if trying to stamp out a black bug. I wiped my stained hand on the seat and tried reading the rest of the paragraph but had to turn the page before finishing.

A few weeks later, I was spending the night at Ruby's apartment in Cambridge. She had tucked me into her brown couch, bundled with blankets and pillows. Soft Christmas lights shone in the corner by the fireplace. Before falling asleep, I meditated on a Taoist verse to quiet my mind. I felt cozy, safe. When I closed my eyes—*BAM*—I was lying on the stiff bunk below deck.

During a phone session, I described these incidents to Irene. "I didn't feel threatened or scared right before they happened. Even on the train, I felt pretty calm beforehand." She told me that the slightest imbalance can flare up a person's PTSD: stress from schoolwork, anxiety about the future, tiredness from lack of sleep, all of which I was feeling.

Visualization can be a powerful healing tool, so Irene instructed me to visualize myself walking out of the ship. My mind drew a blank. I have no memories of stepping onto or off of the ship. I remember standing alongside the ship on the dock in Cambodia, and I remember being on the ship at sea, but I have no memory of entering or exiting.

"I remember *how* I got off, though," I told Irene. Sometime during the nine-day sail, I staggered on deck to attend a class taught by the ship's program director. After the lesson, I stayed behind to talk to him about leaving.

"Being seasick is part of the experience," he said. He told me how his son was chronically seasick but that he lived for the ports. I'd seen his son swaying on the deck, holding feebly to the railing.

"It's not just seasickness," I said. "I don't—I don't know what it is." He looked at me doubtfully.

"I need to leave. When we get to Cambodia."

"But you just got here."

"I need to leave."

He gestured to a map behind his desk. "Wait until Thailand, at least, before you decide whether or not you like the program."

Somehow I knew I would not last until Thailand. And my feeling had nothing to do with liking or not liking the program. The *SV Interlude* was my dream. Yet I had a horrible premonition. If I didn't act, it would become my tomb. Not knowing how to explain myself, I said, "I'm—unhappy."

"You're unhappy? Well then, let's get you off this ship."

That's what it took. Without questioning me or trying to persuade me further, the program director began preparing my departure.

During my phone session with Irene, I relayed this memory to her. "Happiness means feeling like we have freedom," she explained. "The definition of *un*happiness is feeling like we are trapped, cornered. Being unhappy comes from feeling like we have no choices."

Some innate part of the program director must've known the definition of unhappiness, just as some part of me had known to use that word.

"The ship," Irene said, "was your ultimate experience of being cornered. You were surrounded by water. You could not escape. But you listened to your intuition."

So I had.

For our second Christmas together, Luke and I planned a trip back to Montana. We flew into Helena just in time to see Grandstreet Theatre's annual Christmas show. My dad got matinee tickets for the three of us. The play was *Peter Pan*. When we arrived, Luke and I ran into Charlotte in the downstairs lobby. "Wow!" she said. "I didn't know you'd be here for the show." The lobby looked the same, except that new photographs hung on the walls. The collage from *West Side Story* no longer hung by the drinking fountain, photos from *The Crucible* weren't leering over the cookie table, and the *Anne of Green Gables* cast picture wasn't perched next to the greenroom door. We were once the GST kids. Had we been forgotten?

"Charlotte, you remember Luke?" I asked hopefully.

She paused. "Yeah! Of course!" Luke always seemed a little self-conscious about calling himself a Grandstreet alum because he'd only attended the summer camps. Before we set foot in the theatre, I had assured him that people would remember him.

Luckily Charlotte, perhaps a little too enthusiastically, came through. I showed her a photo of Lila on my cell phone. Luke showed her a photo too. Then she glanced at her watch. "Oh! Almost places. We've got to get this thing started." I detected a love of chaos in her voice. The ninety-plus all-children cast was a huge feat to pull off, but year after year Charlotte continued to direct the Christmas shows. "I'd really feel like an empty nester without my kids here," she said, eyes welling a bit. Her daughters, having graduated from college out of state, were now pursuing theatre careers or starting families of their own. Seeing her eyes shine brought me closer to understanding her need for Grandstreet. She didn't do it just for the magic of theatre; she did it for the kids, so that her home would always be filled.

A day before Christmas Eve, Luke planned to meet up with Rory, a friend of his in Helena. Rory had grown up a GST kid too, and now he ran the sound and lights for Grandstreet shows. I remembered him as a gosling in *Honk!* wearing thick glasses and an aviator's cap.

While driving into town, Luke's cell phone rang. "That was Rory. Said he's finishing up at Grandstreet. We'll just meet him there." I was about to object, thinking it might be too emotional to go to the theatre. Everything had gone smoothly when we saw *Peter Pan*, but maybe that had been a fluke. After all, we'd sat in the very last row of the house. I felt wary of getting too close to that stage. Too many memories. Memories I didn't know what to do with.

We parked and walked up to the corbelled entrance of the theatre. Luke opened the polished door and led me inside. Now a young man, but still wearing thick glasses, Rory emerged from the lighting booth and embraced Luke. Bob Westerly, the managing director of Grandstreet, joined us in the foyer. Bob wore a stern face but was quick to giggle. At theatre camp, he used to lead morning warm-ups, making the two hundred campers recite *God Bless Bob Wes-ter-ly, man that we love!* to the tune of "God Bless America."

"Who's this?" he asked.

Luke looked surprised.

191

"Bob, this is Luke. He went to theatre camp here when he was younger," I explained.

"You're probably much taller now, huh."

I laughed, hoping Luke found the joke funny. "Is Charlotte here?"

"No, she flew to California yesterday. Just us here," he said, gesturing to Rory. "Though she would've liked to have seen...you two." While Luke caught up with Rory, Bob and I stood at the back of the house admiring the stage. "You should go up there," he said. "We've changed it some since you've been here."

Luke appeared at my side. "Yeah, let's go up there."

I was torn. I wanted to be on that stage again, but I reminded myself that I'd moved on. I'd found other avenues of expression: hula, teaching, creative writing. Yet, inevitably, they were always compared to my feats on that stage.

Luke escorted me up the stairs to the wooden proscenium. Houselights dimmed as clean, crisp stage lights rose. Together, we stepped onstage. A song began playing over the speakers. Luke held me close and we began slow dancing. I looked up to the rafters, where I had climbed a ladder for my entrance in *Barnum*. I looked upstage left, where I had crawled on for the overture in *Godspell*. I looked backstage right, where I'd leapt onstage for a dance break in *Once on This Island*. On the stage's edge, I'd lured John Proctor into the Massachusetts woods. Next to the proscenium, Charlotte had given me the note to "slow down!" when I'd discovered my dear Ugly Duckling had turned into a snowman. Upstage center, she'd said, "Your eyes just sparkle in this scene." Tears were streaming down my face. I let them soak into Luke's sweater.

As the song faded, he reached into his back pocket. He got down on one knee and opened a small box. "Deme," Luke said, "will you marry me?"

My hands went to my lips. I nodded. "Yes, yes."

The ring shone in a spotlight Bob had set on us. "I can see it sparkle from up here!" he called from the balcony. Rory strolled down the aisle taking pictures of us.

I realized I'd been duped by a bunch of actors.

Luke stood up and slid the ring onto my finger, next to the dolphin one I still wore. "Did you notice the sides?" he asked. I lowered my hand so I could see the edge of the ring. Etched into the band was the Greek key. The meander pattern. The path Odysseus, the quintessential wanderer, followed on his ten-year return home.

Before Luke's proposal, the last time I'd been on Grandstreet's stage was the December Marika took me to meet up with Grace at the sandwich shop. That winter, the alumni were invited back to the theatre to put on a benefit to raise money for summer camp scholarships.

We dragged a couch onto the stage, rolled out a braided rug, and ambled on, clutching mugs of hot cocoa and donning obnoxious Christmas sweaters. Some alumni sang solos, others arranged duets. Some tap danced, played the piano, or strummed the ukulele. I gave a reading of two fiction pieces, a short story called "How to Become an Actress" and my poem titled "Places," the one I'd written in California. Nestled on the edge of the stage in a moose sweater and chocolate brown boots, my words—not the words of a character in a script—swelled to the back of the house. The stage lights felt warm, like flickering embers.

In graduate school, I gained the courage to read my nonfiction writing to audiences. Using my own words—not the words of a character written into a script, not the words of a fictional character I'd made up, but the words of my own life story—I performed in front of classmates, professors, and strangers. I shared how theatre helped a little girl cope with divorce, and how hula fortified my body and soul.

Watching audience members react to my words made me realize that I could help others by sharing my story. What I had guarded, shielded, and kept within me for a decade—out of shame, out of stigma, fear, privacy, or simply out of not being ready—could help others reclaim their own body and voice. I was freeing myself, and, I hoped, freeing others.

When I was nine years old, I learned how to share my emotions and thoughts onstage. I learned how to speak clearly, how to hold still, and how to always keep a pencil handy.

I hadn't forgotten these lessons.

Not every stage is black floor, neon marking tape, and wooden proscenium. After the *SV Interlude*, the stage morphed into dance studios, football stadiums, and theatre camp classrooms. Silence morphed into sentences and paragraphs and chapters. Every day I persuade myself to transform my injury into a blessing.

With every word, I transform destruction into creation.

EXODOS

About a year after starting graduate school, I gathered the courage to look at Oceans Abroad's website. The last time I'd seen it was in January 2004, right before I embarked. The ship on the homepage didn't look like the *SV Interlude*. So I searched "SV Interlude." Several hits lined my computer screen. I discovered that the ship sank off the coast of Morocco in 2008. After enduring one day at sea on life rafts, all of the crew, staff, and students had been rescued.

I waited for a reaction.

The news took a few days to register. Sadness overwhelmed me, then mourning. The *SV Interlude* hadn't been my dream alone. It had been the dream of thousands of students around the globe. It had been their portal to the world too. I thought about Gabe and wondered how he had taken the news. I had an urge to call him, but didn't have his phone number. I hadn't talked to him since leaving for the Philippines, nearly a decade ago. When I returned home, I never e-mailed or called him. I had been too ashamed.

The ship sank on February 17, the exact date I had returned four years earlier. When February 17 approaches each year, I feel a heightened sense of anxiety and grief. Anniversaries are palpable triggers for people who have endured trauma, or for anyone who has experienced loss—of innocence, of trust, of a loved one. The date is there, every year, a number reminding you of what you no longer have and who is no longer with you.

I skimmed through my old notebooks until I came to my journal from 2008. I flipped through the pages until I found the date:

2/17/08 May your spirit be at peace.

I didn't remember writing the entry, but there it was, on its own line. My adventurous spirit must have sensed that the carabiner had finally been unlatched from the railing.

EXTRAS

SOME NOTES

Lariam

In 2009, Roche Laboratories stopped marketing Lariam in the United States. F. Hoffmann-La Roche continues to sell the drug abroad.

Mefloquine

Mefloquine, the generic form of Lariam, is still prescribed in America; however, it is no longer the drug of choice for the US military and Peace Corp. In 2013, the FDA added a black box warning to mefloquine's drug label. In 2015, the CDC announced that mefloquine was no longer effective for the prevention of malaria in Southeast Asia.

Malaria

Malaria remains one of the most prevalent infectious diseases in the world. Ongoing research explores parasite resistance and methods to reduce transmission.

Oceans Abroad

Oceans Abroad continues to operate, now atop the *SV Drusilla*.

FROM PAGE TO STAGE

After enduring trauma, I lost my body and voice. Yet the performing arts helped my feet re-root and my spirit take flight once more. It's only fitting, then, that I share my story onstage too. In graduate school, I wrote a 300-page manuscript. I revised this manuscript into the memoir before you now. Because I haven't yet mastered stillness, I also adapted the memoir into a 90-minute play. *Roots & Wings Onstage* is a one-woman show written, choreographed, and performed by yours truly.

Uniting theatre, dance, and writing, *Roots & Wings Onstage* captures a compressed version of my journey. The play spreads awareness about mental health and offers a story of hope and resilience. Scenes from *Roots & Wings Onstage* are used to educate students and health care professionals about trauma, compassionate care, and art's potential to heal. To schedule an event, visit *www.DemetraPerros.com.*

Praise for Roots & Wings Onstage.

"Demetra skillfully weaves visual scenes, recalled conversations, and medical studies in ways that never lose the audience. Through her honest, human sharing of her own suffering, Demetra becomes an advocate for all who have suffered."

~Robert Lee, MFA
Vietnam Veteran & Author of Guiding Elliot

204

"Those who struggle with mental illness need to know their symptoms are real and they are not alone. The more exposure we can give these 'taboo' topics, the better."

~Mary Middagh, NP
Nurse Practitioner

"*Roots & Wings* shatters the false notion that freedom can be found by suffering in isolation. The parallels that the play strikes in audience members burdened with their own grief or loss evoke the possibility that healing is absolutely within our reach."

~*Maria Stokstad, MC*
Greek American

"*Roots & Wings* not only entertains but also educates. It is art as advocacy, an invitation to reflect on mental health and the conditions that support patients and women."

~Kelly Webster, MA
College Educator

"Referencing ancient mythology, words derived from the Greek language, the statuesque choreography...all brilliant and captivating."

~Vasiliki Agorastos
Modern Dancer

ACKNOWLEDGMENTS

Growing up at theatre school taught me, among other things, that it truly takes a village to produce a show. Likewise for transforming pages into print. I've been blessed with countless keen ears and sharp eyes, most of which were in Boston. In particular, I would like to thank Douglas Whynott for inspiring me to choose this project. His penchant for structure helped me to envision the work, chapter by chapter. I thank Megan Marshall for guiding me through revisions, and for teaching me the power of research. My sincerest gratitude to those I interviewed, whose eloquent words took over the telling of the story when I could not. To my manuscript readers for devoting such time and energy. To Rebecca Demarest for infusing the ancient into the modern. To Patrick and Shad Allan-Scott, whose reverence for the artistic process continues to inspire me. To every backyard, living room, theatre company, organization, high school, university, and Greek Orthodox church that has hosted *Roots & Wings Onstage*. To my parents and siblings, the contemporary Greek heroes. Lastly, an eternal ευχαριστώ to my remarkable husband.

BIBLIOGRAPHY

The research presented in this memoir is not exhaustive. Rather, the following sources were significant to my understanding of invisible wounds, pharmakon, and enduring art.

Gastrointestinal System

Andren-Sandberg, Ake. "Diagnosis and Management of Gallbladder Polyps." *North American Journal of Medical Sciences* 4, no. 5 (2012): 203–211.

Bhatia, Vikram, and Rakesh K. Tandon. "Stress and the Gastrointestinal Tract." *Journal of Gastroenterology and Hepatology* 20, no. 3 (2005): 332–339.

Centers for Disease Control and Prevention. "Norovirus Activity: United States, 2006–2007." *Morbidity and Mortality Weekly Report* 56, no. 33 (2007): 842–846.

Harvard Medical School. "Preparing for a Colonoscopy." Family Health Guide. Last modified August 11, 2015.

Pennebaker, James W. "Psychological Factors Influencing the Reporting of Physical Symptoms." In *The Science of Self-Report: Implications for Research and Practice*, edited by Arthur A. Stone, et al. Mahwah, NJ: Lawrence Erlbaum, 2000.

Greek Art History

Burn, Lucilla. *Hellenistic Art: From Alexander the Great to Augustus*. Los Angeles: Getty Publications, 2004.

Hanfmann, George M. A. "Hellenistic Art." *Dumbarton Oaks Papers* 17 (1963): 77–94.

MacKendrick, Paul Lachlan. *The Greek Stones Speak: The Story of Archaeology in Greek Lands*. New York: Norton, 1981.

Minor, Vernon Hyde. *Art History's History*. 2nd ed. Upper Saddle River, NJ: Prentice Hall, 2001.

Neumeyer, Alfred. "Victory without Trumpet." *College Art Journal* 16, no. 3 (1957): 198–211.

Pedley, John Griffiths. *Greek Art and Archaeology*. 3rd ed. Upper Saddle River, NJ: Prentice Hall, 2002.

Sleeswyk, Andre W. "The Prow of the 'Nike of Samothrace' Reconsidered." *International Journal of Nautical Archaeology* 11, no. 3 (1982): 233–243.

Inspiration

Aristotle. *Poetics*. In *The Rhetoric and Poetics of Aristotle*, translated by Ingram Bywater. New York: Modern Library, 1984.

Barnstone, Willis. *The Poetics of Translation: History, Theory, Practice*. New Haven: Yale University Press, 1993.

Brown, Jason Robert. *Songs for a New World*. Milwaukee: Hal Leonard, 1996.

Cameron, Julia. *The Artist's Way: A Spiritual Path to Higher Creativity*. New York: Tarcher/Putnam, 2002.

Chicago. Directed by Rob Marshall. Santa Monica, CA: Miramax, 2002.

Coelho, Paulo. *The Alchemist*. Translated by Alan R. Clarke. New York: HarperCollins, 1993.

Dumb and Dumber. Directed by Peter Farrelly and Bobby Farrelly. Burbank, CA: Warner Brothers, 1994.

Euripides. *Iphigenia in Aulis*. In *The Actor's Book of Classical Monologues*, edited by Stefan Rudnicki. Translated by Kenneth Cavander. New York: Penguin, 1988.

Fiero, Gloria K. *The Humanistic Tradition: The First Civilizations and the Classical Legacy*. 6th ed. New York: McGraw-Hill, 2011.

Friday Night Lights. Directed by Peter Berg. Universal City, CA: Universal Studios, 2004.

Gage, Nicholas. *A Place for Us*. Boston: Houghton Mifflin, 1989.

Garden State. Directed by Zach Braff. Century City, CA: Fox Search-light, 2004.

Gwynn, Frederick L., and Joseph L. Blotner, eds. *Faulkner in the University*. Charlottesville: University Press of Virginia, 1995.

Harrington, Evans, and Ann J. Abadie, eds. *Faulkner and the Short Story*. Jackson: University Press of Mississippi, 1993.

Melville, Herman. *Moby-Dick*. New York: Penguin, 2001.

Plato. *Six Great Dialogues*. Translated by Benjamin Jowett. Mineola, NY: Dover, 2007.

Tennyson, Alfred Lord. *Selected Poems*. Edited by Christopher Ricks. New York: Penguin, 2007.

300. Directed by Zack Snyder. Burbank, CA: Warner Brothers, 2007.

Tolkien, J. R. R. *The Fellowship of the Ring*. New York: Ballantine, 1965.

Troy. Directed by Wolfgang Petersen. Burbank, CA: Warner Brothers, 2004.

Tzu, Lao. *Tao Te Ching: The Definitive Edition*. Translated by Jonathan Star. New York: Tarcher/Putnam, 2001.

Walker, John. *A Key to the Classical Pronunciation of Greek, Latin and Scripture Proper Names*. London: A. Wilson, Wild Court, Lincoln's Inn Fields, 1804.

Watts, Niki. *The Oxford New Greek Dictionary*. New York: Berkley Books, 2008.

Lariam/Mefloquine

Clyde, David F., et al. "Suppressive Activity of Mefloquine in Sporozoite-Induced Human Malaria." *Antimicrobial Agents and Chemotherapy* 9, no. 3 (1976): 384–386.

Croft, Ashley M. "A Lesson Learnt: The Rise and Fall of Lariam and Halfan." *Journal of the Royal Society of Medicine* 100, no. 4 (2007): 170–174.

———, et al. "Safety Evaluation of the Drugs Available to Prevent Malaria." *Expert Opinion on Drug Safety* 1, no. 1 (2002): 19–27.

Dow, Geoffrey, et al. "Mefloquine Induces Dose-Related Neurological Effects in a Rat Model." *Antimicrobial Agents and Chemotherapy* 50, no. 3 (2006): 1045–1053.

Magill, Alan J. "Special Considerations for US Military Deployments." Centers for Disease Control and Prevention. Last modified July 10, 2015.

Peters, Wallace, and William H. G. Richards, eds. *Antimalarial Drugs I: Biological Background, Experimental Methods, and Drug Resistance.* New York: Springer, 1984.

Public Health Agency of Canada. "Canadian Recommendations for the Prevention and Treatment of Malaria Among International Travellers." *Canada Communicable Disease Report.* 35S1 (2009): 1–67.

Ritchie, Elspeth Cameron, et al. "Psychiatric Side Effects of Mefloquine: Applications to Forensic Psychiatry." *Journal of the American Academy of Psychiatry and the Law* 41, no. 2 (2013): 224–235.

Roche Laboratories Inc. "Lariam: Rx Only." Nutley, NJ: Roche Laboratories Inc., 1999–2008.

———. "Lariam: Rx Only." Nutley, NJ: Roche Laboratories Inc., 2003–2009.

———. "Medication Guide: Lariam." Nutley, NJ: Roche Laboratories Inc., 2003–2009.

US Food and Drug Administration. "FDA Drug Safety Communication: FDA Approves Label Changes for Antimalarial Drug Mefloquine Hydrochloride Due to Risk of Serious Psychiatric and Nerve Side Effects." Drug Safety Communications. Last modified January 19, 2016.

US Food and Drug Administration. "Safety Alerts for Human Medical Products: Lariam (Mefloquine Hydrochloride)." Last modified August 20, 2013.

Posttraumatic Stress Disorder

American Psychiatric Association. *Diagnostic and Statistical Manual of Mental Disorders.* 4th ed. Washington, DC: American Psychiatric Association, 1994.

―――. *Diagnostic and Statistical Manual of Mental Disorders*. 4th ed. rev. Washington, DC: American Psychiatric Association, 2000.

―――. *Diagnostic and Statistical Manual of Mental Disorders*. 5th ed. Washington, DC: American Psychiatric Association, 2013.

Ditlevsen, Daniel N., and Ask Elklit. "The Combined Effect of Gender and Age on Post Traumatic Stress Disorder: Do Men and Women Show Differences in the Lifespan Distribution of the Disorder?" *Annals of General Psychiatry* 9, no. 32 (2010).

Dobbs, David. "A New Focus on the 'Post' in Post-Traumatic Stress." *New York Times*, December 25, 2012.

Karatzias, Thanos, and Zoe Chouliara. "Cognitive Appraisals and Physical Health in People with Posttraumatic Stress Disorder (PTSD)." *Medical Hypotheses* 72, no. 4 (2009): 444–447.

Kashdan, Todd B., et al. "Anhedonia, Emotional Numbing, and Symptom Overreporting in Male Veterans with PTSD." *Personality and Individual Differences* 43, no. 4 (2007): 725–735.

Spoont, Michele R., et al. "Does This Patient Have Posttraumatic Stress Disorder?: Rational Clinical Examination Systematic Review." *Journal of the American Medical Association* 314, no. 5 (2015): 501–510.

Stoudemire, Alan. *Clinical Psychiatry for Medical Students*. 3rd ed. Philadelphia: Lippincott Williams & Wilkins, 1998.

Trauma

Andersson, Matthew Anders, and Colleen S. Conley. "Expecting to Heal through Self-Expression: A Perceived Control Theory of Writing and Health." *Health Psychology Review* 2, no. 2 (2008): 138–162.

Birkerts, Sven. *The Art of Time in Memoir: Then, Again.* Minneapolis: Graywolf Press, 2008.

Burke, Theresa, and David C. Reardon. *Forbidden Grief: The Unspoken Pain of Abortion.* Springfield, IL: Acorn Books, 2002.

Didion, Joan. *The Year of Magical Thinking.* New York: Vintage, 2005.

Doka, Kenneth J. *Disenfranchised Grief: Recognizing Hidden Sorrow.* Lexington, MA: Lexington Books, 1989.

Gilbert, Kathleen R. "Ambiguous Loss and Disenfranchised Grief." Indiana University Bloomington. Last modified August 26, 2007.

Hall, Michelle Flaum, and Scott E. Hall. *Managing the Psychological Impact of Medical Trauma: A Guide for Mental Health and Health Care Professionals.* New York: Springer, 2017.

Siegel, Daniel J. *Mindsight: The New Science of Personal Transformation.* New York: Bantam, 2010.

Smyth, Joshua M., et al. "Prevalence, Type, Disclosure, and Severity of Adverse Life Events in College Students." *Journal of American College Health* 57, no. 1 (2008): 69–76.

Vonnegut, Kurt. *Slaughterhouse-Five.* New York: Dell, 1969.

Walsh, Froma, and Monica McGoldrick, eds. *Living Beyond Loss: Death in the Family.* 2nd ed. New York: Norton, 2004.

AUTHOR BIO

Demetra Perros is a writer, actor, dancer, and advocate. She earned an MFA in Creative Writing–Nonfiction from Emerson College in Boston. Her work prompts individuals, organizations, and communities to talk—out loud—about mental health in America. To spread awareness about invisible injuries, Demetra collaborates with family medicine residencies, nursing programs, pharmacy schools, and health care centers. She visits high schools and colleges around the country to help destigmatize mental illness and to encourage students to find their own sources of persistence. Demetra also shares her work with Greek Orthodox churches and cultural centers to perpetuate ancient art and the immigrant journey. To schedule a performance or workshop, visit *www.DemetraPerros.com.*

Made in the USA
Lexington, KY
29 March 2017